the

PRODUCT
MOMENTUM
GAP

Bringing together product strategy and
customer value.

ANDREA SAEZ & DAVE MARTIN

ISBN 9798862181883

Cover and designs by Hayley Martin.

CONTENTS

A WORD FROM ANDREA AND DAVE

As we pen down the final notes on this book, pausing to reflect on our journey brings a rollercoaster of emotions. It seems like just yesterday that Andrea floated the idea of crystallising our experiences and knowledge into a book. Dave, with his ever-enthusiastic spirit, embraced the idea, and before we knew it, our shared dream had wheels and was speeding down the avenue of creation. (Sorry, not sorry?)

Over the span of a year, this book has transformed, much like a piece of art evolving under the artist's brush. Days turned into nights and nights into days... and sometimes into very long weeks! But as we tirelessly worked on articulating our thoughts, we wanted to ensure that our readers would get the best of what we've learned over our years building products. There was also a non-stop two-week writing flurry during Christmas. Don't worry, we took a break somewhere in between! It wasn't a straightforward journey—far from it. Our initial drafts underwent several revisions, with one particularly intense tear-down that almost took us back to square one. Yet these rigorous exercises in refining and redefining our message only strengthened our commitment to delivering an insightful and impactful book.

Our journey wouldn't have been the same without the keen eyes and brilliant minds of John Cutler, C. Todd Lombardo, Kate Leto and many more. Their feedback was instrumental, shining a light on areas that needed refinement, pointing out nuances we might have missed, and more than anything, ensuring we stayed true to our vision. To them, our gratitude knows no bounds.

Our deepest hope is that this book serves as more than just pages filled with words for you. We want it to be guiding and inspiring you on your journey to building amazing products that are centred on empathy and humanity. Whether you're just starting out or are a seasoned professional, we hope our insights light up your path and encourage you to build products that aren't just great, but transformative.

May you always find the inspiration to innovate, the courage to take risks, and the wisdom to build products that truly matter. And above all, may you always lead with empathy.

Here's to the dreamers, the doers, and everyone passionate about making a dent in the universe. Product is hard, we know. This one's for you.

With warmth and gratitude,

Andrea & Dave

FOREWORD

If you've ever been part of a rapidly growing company that went south, you likely recall that defining moment when things seemed to derail. Something important changed. The team shifted focus from fundamental yet challenging questions like "what behaviors indicate our customers find value in our product?" and "who exactly ARE our customers?" to endless, draining meetings, blame games, and pervasive executive impatience. The team lost its way.

Andrea Saez and Dave Martin aptly term this phenomenon the "Product Momentum Gap." You will not be able to unsee it once you read their play-by-play of it unfolding. If you don't reign things in at this critical moment, it can be hard to get back to the business of building great products and helping your customers do what they need (and want) to do. Act, or it all goes downhill.

But how? By thoughtfully going up and down the stack from business outcomes to customer value and concrete customer behaviors—checking your work, assumptions, and leading indicators along the way.

It's at the exact point that inertia is forcing you to spend less time on the basics that it is most important to keep asking the right questions and map it all out. The reward? As this compact book unfolds, we find increasingly confident leadership teams building on the foundation of their Product VCP (one of a handful of helpful frameworks in the book), tackling the finer points of aligning their teams, measuring progress in customer-centric ways, and framing their strategy more persuasively.

Andrea and Dave have navigated their fair share of HiPPO hazards, bickering boards, and founder freakouts. Interspersed throughout this book, amidst the structured and practical templates and activities, are the stories and anecdotes to prove it. But they do this with much empathy for what it takes to lead a company and write the checks (or deposit them from investors, which is even scarier). They even share their own humbling moments when things didn't go as planned.

Don't let the surface-level simplicity of these methods fool you. What Andrea and Dave have done is describe, in a very accessible way, the full journey from those tense moments of realizing things were going off the rails (and people wondering where all the money was going), to a high-performing, empowered team operating with the support of their leaders and stakeholders.

I'll leave you with a lesson I've learned that overlaps heavily with the ideas in this book. You can't go wrong when you get specific and clear about the humans in the world you are trying to help with your product. The central idea of asking what behaviors—what would people DO—if your product met and exceeded their needs, and using THAT as the anchor point upon which your experiments, roadmap, goals, marketing, strategies, and vision rest will serve you well.

John Cutler

PART ONE
INTRODUCTION

1: ABOUT THIS BOOK

Who this book is for

This book is perfect for anyone involved in leading or influencing the direction of products, including CEOs, founders, product leaders and product managers.

This book was designed not to dictate a rigid approach, but rather offer a flexible path to guide your teams to success while consistently delivering value to your customers. After all, we're building products for others, not ourselves — a common sentiment throughout the book!

If your company already has a product in the market and is seeking growth, this book will help you avoid expensive, if not fatal mistakes.

No matter where you are in your product journey, this book will help you understand the importance of alignment and how product strategy can be harnessed to keep everyone paddling in the same direction.

Leaders who might be struggling to empower product development teams or breaking down silos between product and marketing will find the tools immediately actionable.

Founders and executives who are on their first journey scaling product lines or product teams will learn how to execute strategy and be confident with distributed decision-making.

Those who are challenged with the career-defining dilemmas of relinquishing direct control will discover how strategic alignment and execution are crucial as part of building trust, transparency, and forward movement.

Who we are

From our own collective frustrations, sweat, and celebrations building and bringing products to market, we have seen time and time again teams make similar mistakes that can be avoided.

Andrea has collected expert knowledge from over a decade of bridging the gap between product and customers, in a specialisation now known as product marketing. Working with ambitious startups and scale-ups including ProdPad, Airfocus, and Trint, she has influenced and executed strategy, positioning, and cross-team collaboration. She is a go-to advocate for best-practice product roadmapping and is active in the product community as a speaker and writer.

With over 20 years of experience in the world of product development and leadership, Dave has supported a range of companies including Google, GitLab, Adobe, Snyk, Contentful, BT, Tes Global, Ometria, Evotix and Mention me. He has led new product development from zero to millions of ARR and navigated the complexities of scaling high-growth products. He has played a strategic role in M&A to accelerate product strategy, as well as achieving multiple high value exits.

Why this, why now

With our combined experience and expertise, we've observed common traps that can hinder product growth. One such issue is misalignment across leadership, especially when it comes to the purpose of the product and the value it delivers to customers. With direction constantly changing based on leader reactions rather than evidence, this can have great impact on your numbers, sustainability, and your team's confidence to deliver.

To put it simply: nobody wants to waste time and money, and we want to help you with that.

The book is divided into the sections: Building a Product Value Creation Plan, Creating Alignment, and Driving Action with Accountability.

Each section introduces solutions you can put in place, as well as examples based on our experiences as product leaders.

We believe that this book will help outline the right direction and offer actionable guidance for you and your teams to take towards becoming more aligned, deliver value, and if scaling is your goal, to achieve hypergrowth — all while building products people love.

2: THE PROBLEM: THE PRODUCT MOMENTUM GAP

As early-stage tech start-ups learn more about their customers and what motivates them to buy, teams go through an exciting journey. Usually, these early teams are small and able to react quickly to find early traction, with founders often heavily involved with product development. If you have not experienced it, the pace is incredible. The volume of change in a day feels like weeks in a mature company, and the weeks feel like months. The speed of decision-making is furious, generally with the founder at the helm rapidly adding features and making most, if not all, of the critical decisions.

Guided by the founder, teams have the confidence to build solutions quickly. When they get it right, they have a healthy stream of new customers. The feedback loop from the market is informal but fast. Also guided by the founder, sales teams are continuously busy, and revenue increases quickly.

Fuelled with confidence from the growing volume of customers, the founding team will start the process to raise funds. This is always more effort than anyone expects and is the origin of where things can start to go wrong.

It might seem counterintuitive, but as early-stage tech companies expand, the added resources actually stall their productivity. The more moving parts there are, the easier it is for the leadership team to lose focus. It's easy to get distracted by loud customers, pitch to the wrong prospects, and waste effort on the wrong initiatives.

This slow growth is often painful for the leadership team: the founder might no longer recognise their company or role, while the product leader is drowning in reactive, directionless demands. Meanwhile, investors are concerned that the business targets are missed, adding more pressure on the teams to deliver.

The founder will be distracted, and critical decisions will take longer. There is no longer a direct line to customers on a daily basis, so their learning velocity slows down. And then, all of a sudden, that magical moment happens: funding is secured. It is now all about scaling and expanding, which usually results in hiring.

This frenzy of activity includes hiring sales teams to increase acquisition and customer success teams to increase retention and upsell. There's also a need for more engineers to build product improvements; and let's not forget about product managers to manage the direction and future of the product.

For the founder, it is an exhilarating time with a mix of fear and excitement for potential rewards. Hiring kicks off, and more people are brought on to support the growing business needs. Things begin to speed up as the organisation is hitting the growth curve.

As the company's growth continues, the founder's time is spread thinner and thinner - it is impossible for them to be everywhere at once. They are now less involved in day-to-day product management decisions, which leads them to hire a product leader. If they don't, they risk product development coming to a halt and wasting the investment in the larger, more expensive engineering team.

Given the relatively early stage of the business, it is not

unusual for it to be the product leader's first step into a leadership position. In other cases, the product leader will have leadership experience, but only in established product organisations. Regardless, this is an entirely new challenge; curating a new product function will be unique.

As the leadership team looks inward, they recognise there is no longer a solid understanding of the roadmap, and features aren't being released quickly anymore. The operating cadence has started to slow down. There's confusion over the product strategy, and everyone around the leadership team has their own view of where the revenue is hiding and conflicting opinions on what should be a priority.

Under pressure, sales and marketing will cast a broader net to secure deals. This pressure often leads sales to close deals with clients for whom the product was not designed. Not surprisingly, this is not going to end well.

Meanwhile, the existing customers' product adoption has typically reduced and isn't looking healthy. In the market, competitors are quickly catching up.

The usual symptoms look like this:

- Customers aren't receiving the features they were promised during the sales process.

- Sales cycles are slowing down as competitors offer functionality you don't have.

- Customer service is constantly bombarded with repetitive issues.

- It's challenging for leadership to see how and

where the spending in product development is adding value and boosting business growth.

The pressure on senior leaders is challenging; the business costs have multiplied, while retention and revenue targets are failing. At this point when we often start working with leaders, we ask, "What is the priority: acquisition, retention, upsell or cost control?"

A typical answer a founder might give is, "Everything, we need to stop churn, increase sales, and increase customer lifetime value. We need the NRR (Net Revenue Retention) to double. And we need to extend the runway, maybe even let some people go."

Obviously, if everything is a priority, then nothing is a priority. In these circumstances, nothing has focus, so nothing gets done.

This scenario is almost standard as companies and product lines scale. We have witnessed it time and time again. This is why we give this stage of growing pains a name.

We call this the Product Momentum Gap.

The good news is this can be avoided, and it can be overcome, but only if the leadership team has self-awareness about the issue.

The Product Momentum Gap can be expressed by its fiscal impact on the organisation.

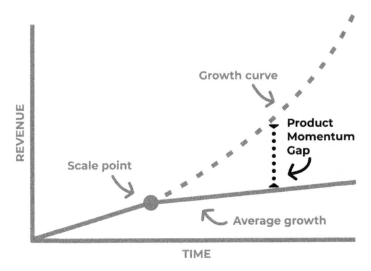

Figure 1 The Product Momentum Gap

The graph above shows the revenue growth of an early-stage company. The company reaches the scale point and forecasts in investor pitches the high growth curve. But the performance plays out to be average growth. The delta between the high growth curve and the average growth is the Product Momentum Gap.

Founders won't always be aware they are in the Product Momentum Gap, but it typically causes leadership to get frustrated as they find that additional resources are leading to underwhelming results. As things get harder, the pressure from the board of directors becomes uncomfortable.

Leadership can feel anxiety over potential issues on the horizon. There is a shrinking cash runway and challenging questions from investors, which sadly results in an all-too-common issue: the company may have to start cutting costs if things don't improve.

This is the point where many founders feel product development is crucial, as it feels this is where the investment funds are being spent. Logically, they must get more involved in the product organisation to bring back successful growth from the early days.

Word of caution: Getting stuck in will likely have a negative effect!

There is a difference between the founder shining a light on product development vs. rolling their sleeves up and getting stuck in. But why?

In the early stages of the company, the founder had high levels of empathy with the target audience (in B2B that would be both the user and the buyer.) It is not uncommon for the founder to have started the company to solve a problem they personally had experienced. As the company grows, the target audience broadens, and the use cases evolve. When the founder jumps back in, they still have the original empathy as their frame of reference, which creates dangerous bias in decision-making. The product management craft is all about discovering customer empathy based on evidence. This reduces bias, allowing the team to deliver a solution that creates customer value. The founder usually did this by instinct, not through a repeatable and scalable product craft.

A good example of this is based on an experience we had working with an EdTech founder who had teaching experience and built a fantastic in-classroom product to help teachers. As the business grew and the target customers changed from individual schools to groups of schools, new problems needed to be addressed.

Throughout the development, there was pressure from the product manager to speak to school groups directly in order to test assumptions. The founder's reply was consistent: "We do not have time". Instead, the founder decided that the best way to speed up development would be for him to make critical product decisions based on their personal experience.

After months of dedicated development, the product was launched but struggled to find its footing in the market. This misstep meant the company missed out on a significant revenue opportunity. One core issue was the founder's lack of first-hand interaction with school management staff. Instead of engaging in genuine product discovery and customer dialogue, there was an inherent bias in their approach. This oversight led to a chain reaction: the product manager resigned and the product leader was dismissed, with the board attributing the product's shortcomings to their decisions. With a subsequent funding round at a less-than-favourable valuation for the founder, the company later introduced a school group product. While it showed some promise, it faced an uphill battle in securing a strong market position.

As a company grows, it's essential to recognize the warning signs that you may be falling into the Product Momentum Gap. Throughout this book, we will share how founders and product leaders can overcome these challenges, scale products effectively, and let go of the reins as you learn to trust your team to do what they're good at.

How do you know if you're about to fall into a gap?

The Product Momentum Gap typically arises from a fundamental misunderstanding of the target customer. This misalignment prompts sales teams to approach prospects with problems akin to, but not quite matching, the target audience. Consequently, sales conversion rates suffer, and those customers who do convert often end up dissatisfied, leading to churn. Without a clear grasp of the target customer's needs, the product development team is left to guesswork, hoping that the features they design will genuinely address the user's concerns.

Misalignment and lack of customer understanding are a dangerous combination, which is the underlying cause of the Product Momentum Gap and the pains it causes.

Bridging the Product Momentum Gap

So how and where can you start to avoid the gap?

The founder requires assurance that the team is prioritising the right areas with the necessary urgency and needs clarity on when to step in to support. The product leader must learn to navigate decisions, even when imperfect, trusting that they're headed in the right direction. Meanwhile, the board of directors seeks confidence that their substantial investment in product development is generating value and will ultimately meet set targets.

It is vital for product leaders to create transparency and alignment while navigating the distractions. Imagine if your team could achieve the following:

- Establish a clear measurable direction to create value, made real through your product roadmap.

- Improved visibility and buy-in throughout the business.

- Streamline decision-making about product development priorities.

- Build a confident product and engineering team that can deliver faster.

- Create a clear pathway to providing exceptional product value, with increased net retention and upsell.

And all of this without the founder needing to lose focus on managing the business by becoming overly involved.

In the upcoming section, we'll present a proven framework designed to accomplish these goals. Named the 'Product Value Creation Plan,' and it comes with a stamp of approval from esteemed venture capital firms like Frog Capital, who advocate its implementation.

3: THE SOLUTION: THE PRODUCT VCP

It is no secret that building products is hard. There are so many things to juggle and so many stakeholders to please, product leaders have to make sacrifices in order to keep moving forward. While this balance of negotiation is sometimes "accepted" — at some point you have to take a step back and ask yourself, do I truly understand what value our product is providing and how it achieves it?

This simple question may be difficult to answer, but often as leadership we get so busy trying to scale the business, that we lose sight of how to scale the product.

As the Product Momentum Gap takes hold, we find ourselves having a harder and harder time figuring out how the solutions we build might help provide value.

This is why we created the Product Value Creation Plan — or Product VCP for short.

This framework connects your product's strategy, objectives, and roadmap, with a concentrated focus on customer value.

After countless coaching sessions with founders and product leaders, we've identified a recurring misalignment between product development and the end user. While the product strategy often outlines the value proposition to the customer, it falls short in defining the pathway to realising that value. This vagueness leaves room for stakeholders to fill in the blanks with their own assumptions. Founders, without explicit agreements, often interpret the strategy in their own way, which may deviate from its original intent.

This isn't exclusive to founders though, sales and technical leaders overlay their own interpretations on the strategy. The aftermath is often a consensus on customer value but a divergence on the product's method to deliver that value. It's a precarious position for the product leader, who might wrongly believe that everyone is on the same page with the strategy.

To align everyone, we need to remove ambiguity around how the product is likely to generate customer value, instead of only focusing on what value it will generate. To do this we have to look at what is directly impacted when we release an update which is a change in user behaviour.

While your product strategy focuses on how to get closer to the product vision, the Product VCP focuses on what user behaviours or actions will create value. The process of building the Product VCP requires focusing on:

- Who are you solving problems for? (Including use cases and personas.)

- Why is this valuable to the customer?

- What experiences do you want to?

- What behaviours or actions will generate value?

- How can you measure the impact your products has on valuable behaviours or actions?

You might be wondering how this is different from a

product strategy. We certainly don't want to be prescriptive with what a strategy looks like or what method to use, but at a high level your product strategy should focus on the following areas:

Outcome: What you want to achieve

- Product vision
- Goals
- Initiatives

Market: Customers and landscape

- Personas
- Competitors
- Technology trends
- Distribution channels

Action: How you will achieve results

- Business models
- Positioning
- Pricing strategy

This seems comprehensive, but some questions remain unanswered, primarily: how do we know where we are providing customer value?

Value is the moment a customer finds a repeatable behaviour that brings a positive impact. The Product VCP assumes an intrinsic link to the company's business goals and repeatable user behaviours. Throughout this book, we will be constantly referring to both value and changes in behaviour as part of the Product VCP.

Emphasising customer value is crucial for any founder or product leader, as it creates a strong foundation for product innovation and sustainable growth. It forces us to go beyond just "build products people love", a catchphrase often used in the product world.

By actively focusing on value, product leaders can identify and prioritise the most impactful problems to solve, streamlining the development process and ensuring that the final product truly resonates with its users. This value-driven approach cultivates a deep understanding of customers' needs and desires, ultimately resulting in products that inspire delight and loyalty. Integrating customer value into the product strategy helps align and motivate teams across the organisation, fostering a shared sense of purpose and vision. This alignment empowers teams to work collaboratively and efficiently, enabling them to design and deliver outstanding products that not only fulfil customer needs, but also drive lasting business success.

Focusing on customer value also helps us deliver on business objectives.

Figure 2 Phases for customer value

In doing that, it means we've got to really understand the intersection between user behaviour, customer value, and business goals.

That's the secret sauce to this whole thing — expressing the strategy in a format that teams can directly understand, measure, and influence.

Ultimately, we need to take responsibility for the fact that the features and solutions we build influence user behaviours.

To align product and commercial teams, and give

designers and engineers tangible targets they can directly impact, leadership needs to shift from a dictated list of features to build focusing on user behaviours that modify or create better user habits. It is these habits that generate value for them, and in turn, growth for us.

Often user behaviours go undiscussed, undefined, or are missing entirely from the product strategy. We need to validate those assumptions and gather as much evidence as possible to proceed with a particular direction, which helps us build exceptional products with the highest impact.

There are four main areas to explore in order to craft the Product VCP. Together these ensure your Product VCP will deliver exceptional customer value while driving business growth. The parts include understanding your target audience, exploring customer value, building valuable user behaviour, and tracking product value creation.

By keeping the following in mind, you can close the Product Momentum Gap and shift your growth curve:

- **Target audience:** Helps teams to understand customers and their use cases.

- **Customer Value Explorer:** Identifies user behaviours that create value for your customer.

- **Value Assumption Builder:** Articulates the valuable user behaviours that product teams can directly influence.

- **Product Value Creation Tracker:** Allows teams to monitor value indicators tracking your product's impact on important user behaviours.

The products that we build will enable, prevent, or encourage certain behaviours, so we need to be very clear about identifying if that modification of behaviours is how we provide value to the user.

Through the course of this book, we will dig down into these parts and provide examples of how and when to use them to close or avoid the Product Momentum Gap across various areas of your company — from OKRs to discovery, to development, so you can empower your team to focus on value and empower their work.

PART TWO

BUILDING A PRODUCT
VCP

1: PRODUCT VISION

When a company or business unit scales, more engineers, designers, and product managers are hired, which causes decision-making to either slow down or become even more distributed. To close the Product Momentum Gap and avoid wasting time and resources, there must be alignment and transparency. Unfortunately, the term "value" is dangerously ambiguous and creates misalignment.

It is easy for decision-makers to get lost in the weeds of feature vs. problem. This often leads to teams building solutions that aren't quite hitting the mark, and even worse, creates confusion with the rest of the team as to why these decisions were made in the first place.

Aligning around the value of product development, (that is, what you're building, and why,) can change the conversation and transform you from a disjointed organisation to one that communicates, collaborates, and works as a single, coordinated and powerful entity.

This means product and marketing working together from the start to understand what and why things are being worked on. This means business-facing teams knowing how to navigate conversations around the inevitable feature requests. And of course, it means leadership being held accountable for the outcomes they produce, not for the number of features they release.

We don't want to ignore the fact that there are a lot of reasons why teams end up going in the wrong direction. There are certainly a lot of contributing factors, like not talking to the customers, silver bullet syndrome, jumping the gun to building features, etc. These and many more are common mistakes — we have seen this first-hand. But we have come to understand there is a root cause that ties all of these together: the lack of a clear product vision coupled with an actionable and measurable product strategy. Frequently product managers know the potential of product vision and strategy to create guardrails for decision-making, but are unable to navigate the influence of sales or challenge the HiPPO (Highest Paid Person's Opinion).

A product vision serves as the foundation upon which your product team and your organisation should make build decisions. This involves having clarity around your target market, what high-level problem you'll be solving for the market, and how you stack against the competition.

After establishing a shared understanding of the product vision internally, it's essential to craft and convey a clear product strategy that charts the course for delivering value. As mentioned previously, this stage often sees a superficial agreement among leaders, as the concept of value remains nebulous and numerous assumptions go unaddressed.

The process of building a Product VCP deepens the alignment of stakeholders demonstrating how strategic initiatives will impact the customer and support business objectives. The founder and other executive leaders will agree on the high-level user behaviours to influence, which will deliver the execution of the product strategy, and in turn the product vision. These behaviours are captured as value indicators to measure value creation, or lack thereof. This allows product development teams to measure their success based on user behaviours which they are directly impacting. Alignment and explicit measures of value closely tie product prioritisation and trade-off decisions to achieve the vision.

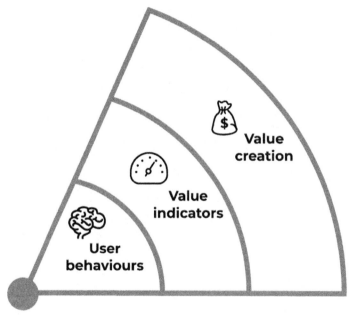

Figure 3 observing value creation

It sounds too good to be true, but consider wrong features are often built when teams don't understand what they're building or why. Features are designed poorly when there is no sense of the experience and behaviours one is meant to influence. The right foundation can help prevent this from happening, and give your team confidence that you're building the right product for the right audience.

With your VCP in hand, you can narrow down the types of problems and solutions you'll be focusing on and identify the target audience for your product.

To avoid the Product Momentum Gap the niche customer segment must be considered a first class citizen. We live in an era of generalist tools that claim to cater to everyone's needs in a single space. The reality is, that if you're trying to do it all and build solutions for everyone, it will likely be useful to no one.

Your strategy needs to answer: who is my product serving next?

Is it for a single-use case? Are you serving teams? Of what size? How does it scale?

By narrowing down these specifics, you'll select your niche and focus on providing value for them. This is key to sustain customer traction. In the earlier phase of the product life cycle, your product appealed to a niche segment; now we must keep the appeal high as we broaden the market and avoid the Product Momentum Gap.

The Product VCP will not do all the research and critical analysis for you, but it will enable aligned and distributed decision-making. Armed with the Product VCP, your product decisions will be scalable and provide value with your strategy and shared learnings, rather than relying on gut feel and an inconsistent approach, which observers might call "luck".

2: THE PRODUCT VALUE CHAIN

As we align our teams, we must make sure we aren't just releasing things because we think they might be right. We need the right level of evidence to understand why a solution is in fact the right one to spend time on.

Realistically, when a feature is released, it doesn't create any value until it is used. As a user adopts the features their behaviour changes, which in turn actualises the value. This is called the Product Value Chain, as illustrated in the diagram below.

Figure 4 value assumptions

Most product strategies fail to discuss user behaviour; instead, they typically consider the value the customer will enjoy and how that relates to the business goals.

For example, a product strategy might describe a key initiative aimed to reduce the customer's operating costs and in turn expect increased payment for this, hence supporting a business goal of increasing revenue.

There is nothing wrong with this, but it is not enough to support distributed decision-making. There are too many value assumptions left for individuals to determine for themselves. There needs to be transparency on which user behaviours or activities the product can impact to reduce operating costs.

A brief example might be a product that handles invoice payments for small businesses. The value assumption could be increasing the speed of invoice reconciliation will reduce operating costs chasing already paid invoices.

The Product VCP extends the strategy to express what change in user behaviour is needed to create customer value. Expressing the desired user behaviour completes the value chain and unlocks the potential for scalable and empowered product development teams.

When product strategy is articulated in terms of user behaviour to create or modify, we are expressing strategy in terms the product development teams can directly impact. The table below illustrates what this might look like for the previous example.

Business goal	Customer value	User behaviour
Increase revenue	Reduce operating costs	Faster invoice reconciliation

Through the process of building the Product VCP, stakeholders debate the value assumption and evaluate the risk of value creation. These conversations align stakeholders, and through clear communication, the product development teams are empowered. Addressing user behaviours removes ambiguity and creates guardrails for innovation to achieve market differentiation and value.

The next chapters will provide a guided process to build your Product VCP. Then we will explore how you can use it to strengthen your product function and grow your business.

It is important to remember this isn't a silver bullet for all possible problems your company may be experiencing. It is, however, a good way to begin aligning your team and think about what value means. Leaning on that to drive changes in behaviour will help your business expand as you target various markets, having a repeatable way of aligning, and re-aligning, while continuously leading with empathy — and of course, showing actual results.

3: MAPPING VALUE

The Product VCP process starts at the top of the value chain — with your business goals — and maps them to customer values. We do this through the Customer Value Mapper.

The aim of the Customer Value Mapper is to focus on the business objectives and clarify the value you believe your customer must receive. These will in turn support the business objectives. If you already have a clear business strategy and a complementary product strategy, you should find completing the Customer Value Mapper relatively easy.

Typically, founders and product leaders possess a distinct understanding of customer values that shape the present product strategy. The aim is not to reinvent the wheel, your current thinking is exactly what the Customer Value Mapper should capture.

Ideally, you should have supporting evidence and high confidence that these customer values will bolster your business objectives. This could come in the way of product research, customer interviews, market research, and customer feedback. If not, we strongly recommend halting here and conducting strategic discovery to boost your confidence levels. This might include learning more about your market, the problems that it's having, and why these matter in relation to your product and the problems you can feasibly solve.

Below is a template showing a diagram of the Customer Value Mapper. It will create more alignment if you complete this in collaboration with peers and senior stakeholders. The boxes are intentionally small to force brevity—but don't be fooled, this doesn't mean less effort is required. As Blaise Pascal wisely noted, "If I had more time, I would have written a shorter letter."

Complete the template collaboratively with the leadership team in this order:

1. Write your business objectives. For most SaaS B2B firms this is some version of acquisition, retention, and upsell.

2. Phrase the benefits you want to create for your customers as customer values. If you have lots of benefits, you may need to dismiss minor values or aggregate them into a bigger value.

3. Highlight why the value is significant to the customer.

4. Armed with the "why", revise the customer values.

5. Draw solid lines between customer values and business objectives to show the primary business objective each customer value supports.

6. Finally, draw dotted lines between customer value and business objectives to show secondary business objectives each customer value might support. note not every customer value will have secondary objectives.

This should be reviewed in line with the company's strategic goals. If there are any changes to these goals, then it is the perfect time to reanalyse how this aligns with the new goals. It is entirely normal and expected for this to be an organic process, constantly updating the more you learn.

Keep in mind that the true value of this exercise emerges from active dialogue among key stakeholders as you navigate through it. While the template serves as a record of alignment, its primary role is to stimulate discussion. Genuine alignment arises from thoughtful debate. This requires founders and product leaders to embrace vulnerability, refraining from merely imposing their beliefs on others. Be mindful of the emotions at play among participants, and choose the timing wisely. For instance, convening right before or after a stressful board meeting might not be the most conducive setting.

Customer Value Mapper™

Business objective:

Business objective:

Business objective:

Business objective:

Customer value:

Customer value:

Customer value:

Customer value:

Why?:

Why?:

Why?:

Why?:

Do you have an example?

If we use the example of a MarTech product supporting customers with content marketing, and explore one branch of the Customer Value Mapper starting with the business objective, a simple mapping might be:

- Business Objective: Acquire £100m of Enterprise customers.
    - o Customer Value: SOC2 standard security compliance
        - ■ Why: Their markets demand high security and the systems we use must be compliant with the highest standards.
    - o Customer Value: Foster audiences of similar interest
        - ■ Why: So our customers can extend and target our partnership offers to drive more revenue.

4: EXPLORING VALUE

Next, we'll use the Customer Value Explorer to clarify each value listed on the Customer Value Mapper, ensuring it aligns with your business objectives.

We start by taking the customer value points from the Customer Value Mapper and examining:

- How would the customer recognize this value?

- What are the customer KPIs? How does the customer measure this?

- What customer actions or behaviours impact the value?

- How could the product help improve these behaviours?

Just as before, these questions are to be discussed collaboratively. Do not try to answer these on your own and present your homework. The conversation needs to be facilitated to get to deeper ideas, and initial reactive answers deserve to be challenged.

Customer Value Explorer™

Customer value:

How would the
customer recognise
this?:

What customer KPI
changes?:

What customer actions
or behaviours impact the
value?

How could Product
improve this?:

Are we best positioned to create this value?:

To further explore these, we can ask ourselves the following question: are we best positioned to create this value for the customer?

Going through these questions can sometimes make the founder feel a bit frustrated, as the answers might seem obvious. However, if they hold back and let others speak first, they often realise that what's clear to them isn't necessarily clear to others. While it's crucial for the product leader to express their views, they should do so without coming off as authoritative. Framing an opinion as a question, like, "Could invoice reconciliation be related to the cost KPI?" can be an effective approach.

By thoughtfully answering these questions, you can determine whether your value assumptions are well-understood, and clarify whether your product can or should solve the problems you're looking to address.

When we examine user behaviours or actions that influence customer value, we're specifically targeting repeatable behaviours. In B2B subscription software, sporadic, one-time values usually aren't desirable. Consistent activities that continuously offer customer value are ideal for subscription-based models, especially in SaaS.

Tackling the question, "How could the product enhance these behaviours?" demands caution. Our brains are instinctively designed to find solutions quickly — it's an energy-saving mechanism. Many individuals find it challenging to piece together the entire puzzle without envisioning a solution. Without a clear solution in mind, discussions can become overly theoretical, risking misunderstandings. This question is posed mainly to ensure everyone is on the same page and to validate understanding, not necessarily to dictate the next steps for development.

Do you have an example?

If there's an adjacent problem you could solve that provides customer value, but it doesn't sit within the product vision and strategy, should you be working on it?

Think of an email service like Mailchimp.

Mailchimp could branch out into "customer communications" and extend beyond email by creating a chat service. While chats could provide value to customers, does it fit within their product strategy and vision? Probably not.

Following this example, it's up to you to determine if the customer value aligns with your business objectives, product vision, and strategy to support problem-solving. Without this alignment, it's easy to fall into the trap of building for commercial potential instead of customer value. The commercial potential will be hard to realise if there is no exchange of customer value. The first approach is about building purely for commercial output, for example, "let's build this for customer x who said they'd pay us a lot of money!" while the latter focuses on ongoing repeatable product growth.

5: VALUE ASSUMPTION BUILDER

In this stage, we'll look deeply into the user behaviours or actions detailed in the Customer Value Explorer. Through focused discussions, we aim to align all stakeholders on the precise user behaviours that the product should nurture to generate value This step forms the backbone of the Product VCP value indicators, leading to high operational effectiveness. As with previous steps, the goal is not just to identify the assumptions but to ensure alignment among all stakeholders.

Start by listing all the user behaviours identified in the Customer Value Explorer that interest you. At this stage, we aren't concerned about granularity or prioritisation we are focused on understanding our assumptions first.

For each user behaviour, explicitly define how it needs to be modified to achieve a bigger customer value. The Value Assumption Builder has space for the assumption and the modifier. For example, if we're looking at the adoption of a certain feature, how might we be able to get the user to change their behaviour to engage with it more? What actions do we need to modify?

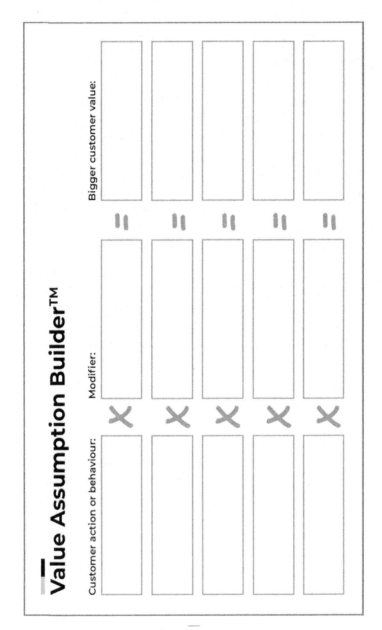

Value Assumption Builder™

Customer action or behaviour: Modifier: Bigger customer value:

For every customer action, there will be a modifier that needs to be in place - that will give us the bigger customer value point we are looking for.

After discussing and refining the list, the next step is consolidating it to a higher level. This is effectively merging related items together and rewording to create a higher-level value assumption.

Finally, with a shorter list, you can prioritise down to a maximum of five items. If five feels too difficult, first challenge how big the impact would actually be for the customer. If required, consolidate further, making it an even higher level.

Stakeholders need to find agreement on the final list. This is where it can be useful to playback the previous steps, helping participants recall the thinking behind it.

It can be tempting for the founder to want all the behaviours, which is understandable, but not overly helpful. Keeping a big list of behaviours means everything is important, leading to a lack of clear priorities. Founders should recall that a primary purpose of the Product VCP is to guide decision-making and instil confidence in the decisions of others. Additionally, the Product VCP aims to empower the product leader to execute the product strategy. Without clear prioritisation, the core objectives of the Product VCP are compromised. It's vital to understand that not all behaviours can be addressed immediately, especially within the scope of a year's focus.

6: TRACKING VALUE CREATION

By now we've clarified the key assumptions of your product strategy that will generate value, translating these into behaviours that provide teams with a clear understanding of how they can directly contribute to value creation. This can significantly enhance the impact of product development, but it requires effective management and support of our teams. To achieve this, we need to measure progress against value assumptions.

We have seen leadership often tempted to revert to top-level business metrics such as "ARR" or "Churn Rate". Measuring these outcomes at the top of the value chain seems appealing as they are significant and likely already being tracked, making it convenient. But if you want to manage and support executing the product strategy, you have to measure what is happening when your product makes contact with the user.

You have to measure value assumptions, and these measurements should come in the form of leading indicators. Lagging indicators take time to materialise, normally at the head of the value chain. They are important in strategic reviews, but useless in day-to-day action. To address any concerns a founder might have about the speed of product development, teams must be equipped with data that facilitates swift and informed daily decisions.

Action needs metrics that provide rapid feedback to inform the next decision. If a feature is released today, you want feedback tomorrow, not in 3 months. Without the ability to iterate, product development will not deliver high-value innovation to support revenue growth. Monthly or quarterly feedback loops force decisions to be based on opinions, many of which will be wrong and very expensive.

Unfortunately, value assumptions are not always easy to align with a leading metric. You need to identify indicators that quickly display the direction of the measurement, even if accuracy is less critical. We call these value indicators — essentially, they are how to measure the value of a feature over time based on our value assumptions. If the indicator is loosely connected to the behaviour, everyone must be comfortable that it would change when the behaviour is modified. A lack of rigour can be uncomfortable, especially for analytical product leaders and many financial leaders who feel a need for a high degree of accuracy. Remember this is there to inform a decision. Without it, the decision is made completely blind.

Start off by clarifying the behavioural change you are measuring, and how the customer value it creates can be tracked over time. Then consider if the customer outcome metric is leading or lagging.

If it is leading, you may want to use this as the value indicator. If it is not, then we need to explore other options.

As always, this is a collaborative process. Work across marketing, sales, and a variety of other teams to identify the value indicator. At the end of the day, everyone needs to understand what and why you are measuring things.

Value Indicator Chooser™

Customer action or behaviour:	What is the measurable value outcome?:	Is this a lead or lag metric?:
Leading indicators:	Can our product impact this?:	Can we measure this?:
Chosen value indicator:		

56

The next step is to understand how features and improvements are performing after a release. This not only allows a product team to understand the impact of their work and learn if they made the right decisions, but it provides leadership and board members the information they need to continue to invest in growth.

The Value Creation Tracker in the next page is a simple report showing the trend of the value indicators that make up the Product VCP.

You can use these figures to evaluate a new release rapidly and support prioritising future work. If stakeholders have bought into the Value Assumptions, we can focus on learning what will improve these metrics.

There are 5 columns on the tracker, each with a different value indicator per row. The first describes the metric, while the second shows the current value for the value indicator with the desired target next. The final two columns show a rolling 4-week change in the value, then a summary showing if it was positive or negative.

Product Value Creation Tracker™

Date upadted:

Value indicator:	Current performance:	Target:	Last 4 week delta:	Trend:

Periodically, for example, every quarter, it is important to review if the lagging metrics are moving in the same direction as the leading indicators. This validates if the product strategy behind the Product VCP is working or not.

For example, let's say that you have retention as a lagging metric on the Customer Value Mapper. If the leading indicator is going up (for example active users,) is retention also going up?

If the lagging metric "retention" is not going up as the number of active users increases, the value assumptions are wrong, which means the strategy is flawed. This will allow you to go back to the drawing board and start again. Believe it or not, this is actually good news! If the value indicators were not being measured, there would be no opportunity to pinpoint what aspect of the strategy was failing. It would be impossible to know if it was poor product execution or problematic strategic planning. When this is unknown, it forces almost impossible decisions onto the founder and product leader.

With the Product VCP, you now have an actionable way of measuring the success of your strategy over time, ensuring you don't fall into stagnation.

As you read on, you will find three distinct sections in the book: Creating Alignment, Driving Accountability with Action, and Selling Value - each focusing on how you can advance your use of the VCP for tangible outcomes. Each section is sprinkled with case studies and real-world examples from organisations that have implemented the VCP, or parts of it.

The final section is a summary of the tools and

templates arranged into the Product VCP toolkit, which is available for digital download at http://www.righttoleft.io/productvcptoolkit

7: ROADMAP TO NOWHERE

To bring this all together, let's consider a real example of a product leader implementing the Product VCP.

Dan worked in a B2B SaaS start-up. Let's call the company HR Tech Inc. The company served the logistics sector in the UK. Dan was the product leader, he reported to the CEO, and was part of the senior leadership team.

The business strategy was clear: sell more to the existing market segment while expanding an adjunct market within logistics. This meant selling to retailers or manufacturers with their own delivery services.

The product strategy defined the target customers and users; it captured core customer values that would justify paying for the SaaS product. The customer value focused on ROI, cost metrics, and average spend per store visitor — and it was all backed up with comprehensive research data. The customer outcome was a powerful combination: to manage costs with a clear increase in packages shipped.

Unfortunately, Dan's work life was highly stressful. The demand from his peers on the senior leadership team came in thick and thin from all angles. His peers had roadmap rage, constantly trying to change plans, and expressing dissatisfaction that their desired features were not being tackled. Perhaps the most difficult was sales, as their budget was falling behind. The CRO frequently made big claims he needed feature x to secure a deal, and without wasting a beat the CEO weighed in and changed roadmap priorities.

Dan had lost all control of the roadmap. Changes were regularly forced on him and he could see development spending was being wasted. To add salt to the wound, those big deals didn't close. In some cases the cost to build the feature was more than the deal size, resulting in high tech debt. Product investment was not delivering a positive return on investment, although the CFO didn't appear to be aware.

The constant changing priorities to please customer success, marketing, and sales resulted in a complete loss of strategic delivery. The customer was rarely the focus, and the market needs were ignored in favour of individual customer's opinions.

As the year-end came around, the CEO reviewed progress with Dan. Needless to say, it wasn't a pleasant experience. The CEO was frustrated that the product strategy agreed on 12 months previously had not been delivered, and he didn't understand why. He naturally felt this was Dan's failure. The last 12 months had been reactive tactical product development and the results were not good. Nearly 50% of the income had been invested in product development with little to no clear attribution to business growth. And without having focused on the needs of the market, the newer features were not even being used.

The company had failed to make any inroads selling to manufacturers or retailers. To make things harder, the CRO was blaming Dan for the shortcomings, saying the product didn't have the key features the new markets were asking for. If this all sounds very familiar, know that it is because it's not an uncommon scenario.

To ensure there was focus, the company decided to use the Product VCP to refocus on the product strategy. Dan and the CEO agreed to revise the product strategy and the governance process driving prioritisation decisions. Unlike previous strategy documents, he did not knuckle down and write the Product VCP on his own ready for a big reveal. Instead, Dan brought the senior leadership team together for a series of workshops.

The first workshop focused on completing the Customer Value Mapper, which took a lot longer than expected. There was constant debate over which customer outcomes supported which business goals. After exploring the different dimensions and agreeing to ignore edge cases, the senior leadership team was aligned.

Naturally, the group tried to jump ahead to the conclusion. They rapidly agreed on which customer outcomes should be the company's priority to achieve their intended market expansion. Dan had to stop the conversation from going too far, as they wanted to allocate resources before having a full understanding of the problem space.

Customer Value Mapper™

Business objective:
Acquire more clients in core segment

Business objective:
Expand market segement

Business objective:
Increase upsell in core segment

Customer value:
Reduce staffing costs

Customer value:
Increase sales

Customer value:
Increase staff retention

Customer value:
Reduce admin effort for optimal schedule

Why?:
Over staffed due to poor demand predictability

Why?:
Staff optimally to reduce time to ship

Why?:
Give staff working hours felxibility

Why?:
Management time burden

Already, after only completing one exercise, his peers were starting to align and drop their personal agendas. But he was aware he still had work to do in order to cement operational change.

In the second workshop, Dan brought his product managers in to join his senior leadership peers to focus on completing the Customer Value Explorer. The product managers' role was to share insight and evidence where needed.

The level of debate was greater than he had expected, but this time it had changed; the market needs were being discussed more. Dan also saw how much knowledge the head of customer service had about the tasks the users were doing and brought quite a bit to the conversation. The discussion was a lot more focused, and edge cases were being ruled out without needing Dan's involvement.

Perhaps most surprisingly, the CEO shared his opinions on which customer values he felt his company was not best positioned to deliver. This was the first time Dan had witnessed the CEO narrowing the product offering, instead of constantly supporting every new idea that was pitched. The mini retro at the end of the workshop revealed a better shared understanding of the problem and an obvious gap in market needs that was preventing growth.

The two workshops had already managed to align the senior stakeholders. But to really make it stick, Dan needed to put the assumptions that had been mentioned at the heart of the product governance.

Customer Value Explorer™

Customer value: Reduce staffing costs

How would the customer recognise this?:

No over staffing
Reduced overtime / supplement payments

What customer KPI changes?:

Staffing bill
Budget overspend

What customer actions or behaviours impact the value?

Staff schedule creation

How could Product improve this?:

Data driven automated scheduling based on demand data
Recommend optimisations
Show budget under / overs for schedule as changes are made

Are we best positioned to create this value?:   Yes

Customer Value Explorer™

Customer value: Increase sales

How would the customer recognise this?:

Smaller queue sizes at peak times

Fewer shoppers leaving without buying

What customer KPI changes?:

Daily packages sent
Packages per picker

What customer actions or behaviours impact the value?

Staff schedule creation

How could Product improve this?:

Data driven automated scheduling based on demand data

Are we best positioned to create this value?:   Yes

Customer Value Explorer™

Customer value: Increase staff retention

How would the customer recognise this?:	What customer KPI changes?:	What customer actions or behaviours impact the value?	How could Product improve this?:
Improved staff morale Staff are better informed on shift patterns Fewer fake sick days due to schedule inflexibility	Staff retention eNPS / Staff surveys	Approving requests to change schedule Sharing schedule with staff	Self serve shift swapping for staff without need for line manager approval. Easily accessible schedule with notifications and reminders

Are we best positioned to create this value?:   Yes

Customer Value Explorer™

Customer value: Reduce admin effort for optimal schedule

How would the customer recognise this?:	What customer KPI changes?:	What customer actions or behaviours impact the value?	How could Product improve this?:
Managers would be more open to schedule changes Managers would spend less time creating schedules Manager & staff motivation	Overtime hours eNPS	Creation of schedule Approval of changes to schedule	Automated schedule proposal Automation of changes Automated rotation of less favourable shifts (removing accidental bias)

Are we best positioned to create this value?:   Yes

The next workshop took the customer outcomes and enabled the team to define value assumptions. This workshop moved quicker, the discussion was faster, and agreement was found more naturally.

Defining the desired user behaviours showed many in the team supported multiple customer outcomes. The behaviours surrounding the market needs gap were fewer than previously thought.

The team had many value assumptions at first, but with some healthy discussion, Dan managed to get this reduced down. He then went back to the Customer Value Mapper and plotted the value assumptions so the group could see which business goals each impacted. The discussion removed more value assumptions, leaving just 8 on the table.

A discussion was then led to understand the impact of not delivering on each of the 8 assumptions, highlighting that only 5 really mattered.

The CEO approved that those 5 should be part of the product's strategic focus.

The company had a clear product strategy and agreed focus. Most importantly, all the leaders were aligned and had started self-filtering low-priority ideas. But Dan was not finished!

Value Assumption Builder™

Customer action or behaviour:		Modifier:		Bigger customer value:
Optimise schedule based on demand	X	Optimised at a weekly level	=	Reduce staffing costs
Optimise schedule based on demand	X	Faster	=	Reduce staffing costs
Review budget overspend	X	Earlier / faster in workflow	=	Reduce staffing costs
Review budget overspend	X	At a daily level	=	Reduce staffing costs
Review schedule budget forecast	X	Daily view	=	Reduce staffing costs

Value Assumption Builder™

Customer action or behaviour:		Modifier:		Bigger customer value:
Optimise schedule based on demand	X	Optimised at a weekly level	‖	Increase sales
Review schedule budget forecast	X	Daily view	‖	Increase sales
Shift change approval	X	Faster	‖	Increase staff retention
Staff view schedule (or part of)	X	More frequently	‖	Increase staff retention
Requesting a schedule change	X	Easier / faster	‖	Increase staff retention

Value Assumption Builder™

Customer action or behaviour:		Modifier:		Bigger customer value:
Review for approval cost impact of schedule changes	X	Faster	=	Reduce admin effort for optimal schedule
Create schedule	X	Faster	=	Reduce admin effort for optimal schedule
Review budget overspend	X	Faster	=	Reduce admin effort for optimal schedule
Create schedule	X	With less bias	=	Reduce admin effort for optimal schedule
	X		=	

The final workshop proposed leading indicators to track the progress around the value assumptions, and mapped them to lagging performance metrics further down the value chain. This resulted in 5 numbers to use as the basis of a prioritisation scorecard. It provided Dan measurable leading indicators to use in order to manage his team and inform prioritisation.

From that point on, Dan reported on the metrics regularly in the senior management meetings. His commitment to the board was impacting the metrics on the VCP, not delivering features on a roadmap. If his team learned a roadmap item was not going to move the numbers as much as expected, they were empowered to make better decisions.

Six months later, Dan reviewed the value indicators against the lagging performance indicator, for example Churn or ARR. The performance looked good; the value indicators had increased. New features were being used by new customers in the new segment they were trying to break into. The value being created by the product had significantly improved that year.

There was something to keep an eye on though — not all the linked lagging metrics had gone in the right direction. Upon exploring the reasons for the underperformance, the conclusion was that one value assumption was wrong — it was not the root cause of the desired outcome.

Dan adapted the product strategy and the VCP to reflect the new strategic learning. His team revised the roadmap and pivoted their plans, saving them from wasting significant resources and creating new opportunities.

Dan's morale was far higher, as was his team's. He was still busy but managed the frustrations far better and finally felt part of the wider leadership team.

8: HOW TO MAKE THIS HAPPEN

Product managers often get stuck wanting to please everyone — and often "everyone" results in neglecting the most important group: your own customers. The role of a product manager is a difficult one and it is full of unknowns.

Building the Product VCP to set direction for product teams in terms of user behaviour removes a layer of uncertainty for the product function.

The two most important things you can do for your team are:

- To bring the focus back to the purpose of why your product exists by using the product vision.

- Continuously promote a culture of learning and accountability by using the Product VCP value indicators.

Leadership want their companies to scale and be successful, but this requires increased distribution of decision-making. If all important decisions have to be made or approved by the leader, the size of the company is limited to the decision-making bandwidth they have. To make matters worse, if solutions are dictated by leadership, it kills alignment, destroys transparency, erodes trust, and demotivates staff.

As such, prioritising alignment with everyone so all the great talent is paddling in the right direction must be the number one focus. If you don't focus on this, no one else will! Just a few misaligned engineers create a phenomenally destructive impact. A top tip is not to miss out on the power of building the Product VCP inclusively and cross-functionally.

Using the Product VCP, product strategy is articulated as achievable and measurable goals focused on the user that provide a high-level view of how the product will support the vision and accomplish business objectives. It brings together who the product is for, the needs of the market, and your set business goals. Without a product strategy, you risk having no alignment on what approaches product development will take to iterate closer to the vision and deliver commercial goals.

Research across thousands of products by the analytics platform Pendo found that 80% of features released are rarely or never used. This figure suggests significant waste in product development and enormous lost opportunity. Rapid experimentation and learning are crucial if your product development investment is going to create features your users will adopt. If a user fails to adopt a feature, it is impossible for the feature to create value.

If product managers are to create market differentiation and a product in high demand, they need to be accountable for the user outcome they create.

PART THREE
CREATING ALIGNMENT

1: TRANSFORMING TO STRATEGIC OUTCOMES

What happens when the product development organisation is aligned, taking positive action, and has clear accountability?

To answer this let's review an example, this time a highly successful B2B SaaS company helping companies with compliance. They had enjoyed a minimum of 40% year on year growth for the last 8 years and reached a 9-figure revenue line. The key to their growth had been the ability to satisfy market needs faster and more comprehensively than their competition.

As their market matured and competition caught up, there were fewer obvious, underserved needs for their customers. The strategy of continuing to digitalise previous offline processes was drying up, and the leadership team were seriously concerned about future growth. They recognised it would require innovation beyond migrating the paper process to the digital process.

Their leadership team understood that continued growth rates would require a different product development approach compared to what had fuelled their past success. They believed there was a need to become laser-focused on creating innovative solutions for their customers' most challenging problems. They knew they had to think differently about how customers recognise and realise the value from using their products.

The endeavour they undertook involved reshaping their product strategy, giving product development teams a renewed purpose and adopting a learning culture to drive innovation.

They knew what good looked like: they wanted outcomes over outputs, they wanted high-velocity experimentation, and they needed rapid iteration and innovation. The C-suite bought into the idea of empowered cross-functional product development teams, but they had heard of other companies failing to adapt and moving backwards while trying to transform.

This is where they called for help to embrace the Product VCP.

At the start, the existing product vision was not strong enough to form a foundation for the Product VCP. The first effort was to rewrite the product vision and focus it on the product experience. After working through a few iterations, a new and inspiring product vision was formulated.

Leadership then got to work with the product managers to build out the Product VCP. The team quickly identified jobs to be done but needed the VCP to give clarity and define how the customer's perceived value would grow using their products.

The CPO found the Customer Value Explorer or CVE is the key to providing clarity. Using the CVE drove the right conversations to shape assumptions around and which user behaviours would be game changers. Focusing the thinking on the behaviours instead of the solutions allowed for deeper connection to the business plan. The conversation switched from which feature should be built to what behaviour might drive growth.

The value assumptions provided the product team

clarity. They were able to explore different product discovery techniques and more deeply understand problems. In the early days, they felt the Product VCP was key to being outcome-focused. Articulating the strategy using the value indicators has informed OKRs, linking quarterly action directly to the strategy. Talking to the CPO, they said, "most importantly the focus on modifying customer behaviours has given us confidence our product development investment is delivering maximum customer value." The impact of their results had increased adoption and supported new sales, leading to strong year-on-year performance.

Their confidence also grew over time. A board review of the Product VCP alongside lagging business metrics showed value indicators in the Product VCP going up as the related business revenue and churn metrics improved. While it is true this might not be causal, it provides a new injection of confidence.

The CEO now holds the CPO accountable for the Product VCP metrics. Instead of being measured based on the delivery of output, the CPO is held accountable for outcomes directly impacted by the product, with clear alignment across the C-suite and board to how it supports the business goals.

The CEO agreed to manage the product leader based on the outcomes they had aligned themselves on as part of the Product VCP. The C-suite conversations around the product ceased to be about what feature will land when. They stopped creating solutions in the boardroom, which was contributing to the disempowering of the entire product development team. Over a 12-month period, the perception of changing the roadmap moved from failure to success. Changing the roadmap is now positively viewed as saving the company from wasting capital.

The effect of using the Product VCP at the top of the business removed any hiding places for the CPO and created increased focus on strategic impact. The venture capital board directors now understood the high-level justification for product investment and were able to clearly understand the product investment decisions. With more clarity on where strategic bets are being placed, board-level product decisions became bolder, yet with clear focus.

The company had great success and just before this book was published, enjoyed a positive exit to an acquirer.

In the next section, we will explore how the Product VCP can be used to support articulating product strategy, aligning the organisation, value-focused prioritisation, creating transparency, and building accountability.

A business that has alignment, action, and accountability is fully prepared to avoid the Product Momentum Gap and achieve their targets, leading to success.

2: ARTICULATING YOUR STRATEGY

A product strategy defines how product investment will get closer to the product vision. The product vision will achieve the business goals, and it is intrinsically tied to the business strategy. Being able to articulate a product strategy clearly can make a world of difference, providing alignment across your organisation.

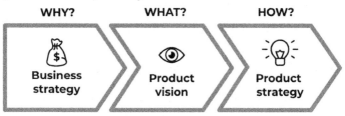

Figure 5 Path to product strategy

To ensure that your product strategy is effective and well-understood, it's crucial to focus on three key aspects when explaining it:

- **Why** is it important to the business?

- **What** value will the customer get?

- **How** will the product deliver that value?

The company's product strategy usually covers the "why" and "what", while the "how" is often relegated to the product roadmap. This approach can be problematic. To better understand this, let's look into the two tools that are crucial for communicating decision-making throughout the organisation: the product strategy and the product roadmap.

These tools should provide a dynamic direction, flexible to change based on evidence and circumstances. Treating them as static, immutable documents is counterproductive. Articulating the "how" using the product roadmap forces the wrong conversation for strategic planning and investment decisions. The discussion often devolves into specifics about features and deadlines, neither of which are beneficial for strategic planning.

Misusing the product roadmap to explain the "how" forces product development teams to provide made-up answers to impossible questions, like stating delivery deadlines they know they won't reach. This approach can lead to misguided business decisions and false promises, undermining trust and morale while misdirecting investments. There is no way a year of pre-planned features will give you the insight you need to understand desired outcomes.

The reality is markets change, customers grow, and industries shift — we cannot expect a roadmap to remain static without evolving based on new evidence. The more we adhere to solutions without being flexible, the more we run the risk of not being able to respond to changes quick enough to stay competitive. We need to be able to give ourselves the space to change the solution if it's not working.

Let's be clear here, the issue isn't the roadmap itself, but how it is being used. Instead of blaming the tool, we need to reframe how we articulate the delivery of product value expressed through the product roadmap. To do this, we first have to consider the foundational impact of releasing a feature.

Releasing a feature might impact our costs, our completion of an RFP, legal compliance, or user behaviours. As such, we need to think of the "how" as high-level user behaviours that will be modified or created in some way. This bridges the gap between strategy and execution described by the roadmap and allows it to be far more fluid.

Measuring these behavioural changes provides accountability for strategic action, separating the roadmap from set features and deadlines. A well-articulated product strategy empowers teams to find optimal solutions, accelerating time-to-market, and increasing the return on product investment.

At the end of the day, being able to build better habits is the value that users are looking for — and that is the biggest driver for growth. Ensuring accountability of the creation of user behaviours avoids the pitfalls that lead to the Product Momentum Gap.

3: ORGANISATIONAL ALIGNMENT

We all know what a business vision is and the importance behind it, but did you know you also need a product vision to support your team moving forward? Many companies make the mistake of using the same document for both, which blurs the lines between what the business aims to do vs. what problems the product aims to solve.

To prevent confusion, create a separate product vision that supports your business strategy, guides your product strategy, and unites your team around a shared set of values and goals.

Business ≠ Product

It's crucial to recognize the differences between your business and product visions, even if your company only has one product. At a high level, your business vision will answer the following:

- Who you are

- What you do

- Why you do it

- What the business goals are

This focus is on your company's values and mission, irrespective of the number of products it may develop now or in the future. In contrast, your product vision will highlight the following at a high level:

- Who the target audience is

- What is the concept and experience of the product

- What are the key benefits

- Main competitive advantage

A product vision emphasises the customer, the product and its key benefits, and what the main competitive advantage is, separate from the business's values and strategy. A good product vision will inspire people to why your product is meaningful.

Let's consider Hubspot, a well-known B2B company focused on CMS and operations for sales and marketing teams. Their product vision explains what is different about them, and focuses on the experience of an all-in-one platform:

"The world has changed, and it's time to transform how you market and sell to match how people shop, buy, and share experiences online. That's why we built HubSpot. With HubSpot's award-winning inbound marketing and sales platform, you will attract more visitors, generate more leads, and delight more customers: all in one platform."

The full vision is available in a YouTube video and explores the experience based on specific use cases.

Empowering your team

New employees often begin with enthusiasm and curiosity, but find their organisations inadvertently stifling this energy with restrictive processes and systems. With an added controlling mentality, fearful workplace cultures take power and energy away from people, even for top achievers.

People don't require permission to accomplish great work, but rather a fearless culture that supports risk, encourages brave talks, and promotes learning and experimentation.

Empowered teams not only have the flexibility to be more innovative but are able to solve problems that provide real value and positive impact to the business. Empowerment leads to autonomy, and with greater autonomy comes a boost of motivation and self-directed work.

Clear product visions will empower your teams to innovate and find amazing solutions for your customers. Make sure you're being transparent about the challenges and opportunities, as opposed to dictating on specific features.

Think of it this way:

- A challenge is a problem that your target market has. What opportunities does your product have to be able to solve that in a helpful way? Write this down without committing to any features upfront.

- If you start off by writing down the solution or features right away, you are restricting your product development teams without having the opportunity to explore if there are better ways of solving the problem in the future.

- It's important to give teams room to explore, run discovery, and tackle challenges in various ways to create market-leading products. The more flexibility you're able to provide, the more ingenious the approach to problem-solving will become. This will help you avoid becoming stuck on the average growth curve of the Product Momentum Gap.

Breaking down silos

A common issue in scaling companies is a lack of communication and collaboration, which can lead to assumptions about decisions, direction, and product definitions. This often results in the product roadmap being treated as a tactical document, rather than a set of potential steps to execute the strategy.

It's important to remember that the business and product visions should complement each other. They might be two separate documents, but they don't exist in vacuums. Together they play crucial roles in guiding your team and organisation towards success. Be sure to share and explain your business strategy, product strategy, and product roadmap with everyone to empower, align, and unite your direction and focus.

4: CREATING TRANSPARENCY AND TRUST

Team members can have different views about the best way forward. I'm pretty sure you've all experienced this: a situation where you start with a vision, a set of goals, and some high-level ideas. Yet somehow, everyone in your team has a slightly different view about how things should be approached.

This in itself is a problem, but it can be worse when some of those views end up being dramatically different. This in turn causes teams to become distracted, and as we attempt to fix things, we inadvertently create even more distractions.

Product leaders, this is where you come in. If you don't have your team aligned, or your strategy aligned — how on earth will you have your roadmap aligned? Even more so, how do you expect to create an atmosphere of transparency and trust when you're opening yourself up to constant change of direction and misalignment?

Setting direction without dictating solutions

Before we get on talking about roadmaps, let's start from the beginning: in order to have a roadmap, we need to make sure that we have a strategy and a direction.

When defining strategy, be sure not to confuse "setting direction" with "dictating solutions". Solutions may not work and will need to flex to solve the problem. Solutions need to be tested in the real world with the customer. This can be particularly challenging for founders who might have previously enjoyed the creativity of "solutionising".

If the strategy dictates the solution, and it's being built at a high level in the leadership group, leaders will end up doing the work of product teams. This means they will make decisions based on little to no evidence, which results in feature bloat and lack of value for the customer. This risk is not going deep enough to the problem to deliver a solution correctly and will result in wasting cash-building features that fail to gain market share or retain customers.

As a company grows, matures, and evolves, it needs to be able to support decisions and mitigate risks by thoroughly understanding why those decisions are being made in the first place. For B2B companies experiencing growth, one big challenge is being able to remove the founder from solely making these decisions. As we've discussed earlier, this is not uncommon in the early stages of the company, where they were product manager and product leader. As the organisation scales, it's sometimes hard for the founder to realise they can't do this anymore, and they need to let go of this and trust the people they hire to make those decisions.

The reality is that founders and leadership will be increasingly removed from speaking to customers every day. As this change comes about, the structure of relationships evolve — as does the process of discovery and evidence and the opportunities that are uncovered.

The Product VCP creates a high focus on value assumptions to help the founder have confidence and set teams up for success.

Aligning strategy to value

As part of the leadership team, you should be able to empower your teams with strategic direction so that they can build amazing products. A clear, well-understood strategy enables teams to tackle customer-centric problems and make impactful investments.

Conversely, a well-defined but not well-understood strategy leads to reactive, tactical decisions. Imagine having spent hours and hours crafting a well-thought-out strategy that is then not used by your teams. This can be incredibly frustrating!

How you solve this problem is with the Product VCP. It ensures alignment between the product strategy and customer value delivery, removing ambiguity in decision-making. It answers some of those "whats" and "whys" behind decision-making, ensuring that there aren't question marks or blank spaces that are open for interpretation.

Articulating strategy on the roadmap

Once the direction, strategy, and value are aligned, they should be articulated in a product roadmap. And this is where things get really interesting.

Often, that strategy is expressed as features rather than outcomes based on the value we are trying to provide the customer. This results in a list of solutions to build and leads us to being less aligned with strategic thinking. **Solutions are commitments**. They are hard to change and very limiting.

Don't build a roadmap to nowhere. Instead, focus on

outcomes that empower teams to explore various solutions and gather evidence to inform decisions. Without value, we're merely building unwanted features.

And this is how it all comes together: A solid vision supplemented by a product VCP will help your entire team understand how the strategy is aligned with customer value. This in turn empowers you to create a roadmap based on outcomes, instead of a list of solutions based on no evidence. This not only helps prevent the risk of business failure but sets you on the path to positive adoption and hyper-growth, allowing your teams to build products people love.

This clear transparency provided to all of your teams about what, why, for whom, and how decisions are being made will lead to a supportive internal community that is able to back each other with the utmost confidence.

5: HOW TO MAKE THIS HAPPEN

Leadership is there to create alignment and purpose.

This sounds simple enough, but it is far more complex than one would think. To help product success, it's important to remember you're not there to support an individual's hobby ideas; you're not there to make excuses for toxic behaviour; you're not there to have all the answers. You are more useful off asking questions, and you definitely are not there to be right all the time — vulnerable leadership is powerful!

Gut feeling can often lead decision-making processes, which isn't inherently bad. However, it's vital not to let it obscure the need for data and experimentation. Instead of directing your team based on instinct alone, integrate your ideas with the experimentation process. This will enable you to verify whether your gut instinct aligns with empirical evidence.

This shifts your focus from the solution space to the problem space. From here, you can formulate hypotheses and design experiments to test them. The data from these experiments will not only guide your decisions but also boost your confidence in the direction you're pursuing. Remember, being proven wrong is part of the process. Embrace it. After all, the purpose of experimentation is to mitigate business risks and support the creation of superior products.

Reminding your team of the value they're providing is equally important. The Customer Value Explorer is designed to understand how customers perceive value and to define user behaviours that contribute to this value. This isn't about detailing granular tasks, but rather about identifying impactful high-level goals, projects, actions, or emotions.

The product, customer success, and sales teams will all have input into what these behaviours look like and how they support the desired customer value. You must open up your team to these ideas, socialise them, and consolidate them into concise descriptions.

The last ingredient in this recipe for success is trust. If you cannot trust your teams to learn from the process, they never will have the confidence to make mistakes. We spend our entire childhood being told that making mistakes is a bad thing. Product is the opposite of that. Life is the opposite of that!

You need to trust your teams to learn from the process, and they need to feel confident enough to make mistakes. Shifting perspectives, especially when transitioning into a leadership role, is challenging. You not only have to encourage others to unlearn certain habits but also offer the necessary support and provide a safety net. Establishing a trust-based environment has a domino effect: your teams will be better equipped to combat imposter syndrome, make a more significant impact through their solutions, and promote innovation.

Of course, trust is not the same as blind faith, and we still need to provide guidance as much as possible. The Product VCP sets guardrails and controls to allow trust to be fostered without losing sight of direction, intention, and vision.

PART FOUR

DRIVING ACCOUNTABILITY WITH ACTION

1: INITIATIVE PRIORITISATION

A good product strategy has depth and covers multiple dimensions to deliver organisational success. Often lengthy and detailed, not all individuals can fully grasp every facet of the product strategy. This complexity can hinder the initiative prioritisation needed to execute strategic goals. The pressing question, which often nudges companies towards the Product Momentum Gap, becomes: 'How can we efficiently determine if an initiative aligns with our strategic value?'

The Product VCP clarifies value assumptions and highlights user behaviours that the product strategy aims to influence. Remember from earlier chapters, value assumptions are beliefs or hypotheses about how a product will create value for the customer, and subsequently support the company's business goals.

Value assumptions operate at two primary levels in the value chain:

1. Product Impact Value Assumptions: These assumptions are about which user behaviours — initiated or modified by the product features — will create value. In simpler terms, they answer the question: *"How do we believe our product features will change user behaviours in a way that creates customer value?"*

2. Strategic Value Assumptions: These assumptions deal with how the perceived customer values, resulting from the behaviour changes, will support the company's

overarching goals. This can include things like a customer's willingness to pay for the perceived value. These assumptions essentially answer the question: *"How do we believe the value perceived by the customer will further our company's goals?"*

It's crucial to clarify and validate these assumptions.

Misunderstanding or misinterpreting them can lead to high-risk product investments resulting in residence in the Product Momentum Gap. A lower-risk approach is to deeply understand these value assumptions, be clear about them, and ensure that the leadership and key stakeholders are aligned around them. When there's alignment on value assumptions, it can benefit many functions of the company, including product development, marketing, customer success, and sales. (More on that in the chapter "Selling Value").

With alignment on value assumptions, we can direct our operational efforts towards user behaviours. The Product VCP is conveyed as a list of leading metrics that signify the status of user behaviours of strategic interest. For effective operational execution, these metrics should be leading and not lagging, enabling product teams to learn from the impact of feature releases.

Depending on the user behaviour, the metrics may have to be a guiding indicator instead of a direct measure. We call these metrics "value indicators," and share the Product VCP as a table.

Improvement in value indicators implies that the product is positively influencing user behaviour. If our value assumptions are correct, the user behaviour creates customer value, which in turn impacts our business goals. Consequently, the product team can operationally concentrate on the value indicators.

Obviously, in line with a strategic review (which is not a weekly or monthly event,) the value indicators should be reviewed and cross-referenced with lagging indicators and qualitative data to reinforce confidence around the value assumptions, and highlight any that need revision.

When it comes to prioritising, it is well known that there are a variety of prioritisation frameworks available. The aim of the Product VCP is not to change what you're currently using, but rather to ensure strategic value is prioritised and ad hoc distractions are purposefully chosen with a clear understanding of lost opportunities. The Product VCP encourages prioritising opportunities, not features.

Whatever framework or method you use to prioritise, there is usually an estimate of value included. It might not always be explicitly called "value"; for example, in the framework RICE, "Impact" equates to value. How value or impact are estimated is typically not standardised. This introduces significant bias into the process, with the loudest voice or last customer conversation influencing prioritisation. Without a definition of value, prioritisation quickly becomes reactive and tactical, leading to missing strategic opportunities and widening the Product Momentum Gap. Ineffective prioritisation is a root cause of average growth in product companies. The good news is this can all be resolved using the Strategic Value Matrix.

The Strategic Value Matrix is a scorecard to change impact or value to be strategic. There is a more complicated version which includes weightings for each value indicator, but for now, we will stick with this version. The scores for each item being reviewed will then be added to your existing prioritisation method.

Strategic Value Matrix™

Value indicators:

Strategic bets:

Total

The matrix has a row for each item to be evaluated, referred to as strategic bets and columns for each value indicator from your Product VCP.

For each strategic bet or possible roadmap item, evaluate the size of the impact or value for each value indicator. We prefer a score with a range between -1 to 2, with -1 being the value being destroyed and 2 being the significant value being created. If you are unsure what large looks like, consider the Product VCP Tracker, which has targets for each value indicator.

When you have scored each indicator for one strategic bet, add them together and put the answer in the total box. This figure is the number you will plug into your prioritisation framework.

2: BACK TO BASICS WITH OKRS

If you want teams to make sound decisions that align with strategy and business goals, it's essential to clarify those goals. Inadequate goal setting will result in inadequate decision-making and risk driving the business into the Product Momentum Gap.

Many companies adopt management frameworks such as OKRs to create focus, but misused OKRs can be the cause of distraction, misalignment, and poor decision-making.

For example, saying that your objective is to "become the leading product in the industry" with a key result of "1000 new users every month" is ambiguous and can be misleading.

At first glance, this OKR might seem reasonable. But it's flawed in several ways. The objective is vague and doesn't quantify what "leading" means. Meanwhile, the key result is a vanity metric. Without understanding user behaviour or ensuring these users are active and getting value from the product, this metric doesn't provide a clear picture of success.

How can a framework designed to help give you focus also completely derail you? More often than not, we convolute business and product objectives into one, leaving little space for teams to be autonomous and empowered to solve problems. This is where the Product VCP can help create a distinction that aligns both sides well. When we're thinking about how the Product VCP relates to product strategy and product vision, it might look something like this:

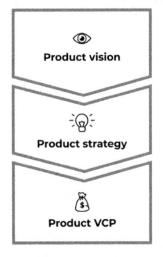

Figure 6 Vison to Product VCP

Objectives cascade from the business down to the product level. While OKRs help phase and execute your strategic plans, the VCP helps you define the right OKRs, showing you're providing value within a particular problem that is being solved and executing the product strategy.

Example of a poorly defined product OKR:

- Objective: "Make our platform better."

    o Key Result: "Increase session time by 20%."

This OKR is problematic because "better" is subjective and doesn't pinpoint a specific area of improvement. Additionally, longer session times don't necessarily indicate a "better" platform. Users might be spending more time because they're confused or unable to find what they're looking for.

It's important to understand and be aligned on what your business objectives are. Once leadership has aligned around those, then the product team can start defining strategy bets which will deliver to the Product VCP.

Increasing Annual Recurring Revenue is also not a product objective. The direct outcome of your product will not generate more revenue — that's the outcome of your business. Generating revenue takes marketing, sales, customer support, and product. Your product's objectives and key results should focus on building customer value by creating or modifying behaviours for your users.

While business OKRs like increasing ARR represent the broader organisational ambitions related to growth and revenue, product OKRs delve into the granularities of user experience, feature adoption, and product quality. Both are intertwined — a stellar product can lead to increased revenue — but their focus areas are distinct.

A well-aligned organisation ensures that the product team's drive to deliver value doesn't clash with the company's overarching financial and growth goals. By understanding this distinction, teams can navigate the challenge of translating broader business objectives into tangible product improvements.

Once leadership has outlined business-level objectives as clearly as possible, it is time to understand how to measure success, with the product VCP helping you evaluate the different strategy bets.

These strategic bets will be tied to value indicators, which are then tied to objectives mapped to specific user behaviours you're looking to change.

For a moment, let us think about a very real situation we regularly see — building a new feature vs. improving the awareness of the existing feature as it is. Which one might you start with? Before we jump to any answers, let's start from the top.

Suppose we are looking at a company that is building a product providing users the ability to edit and manage different types of content, like audio and video. They have found themselves with a problem, their users don't know they can process high volumes of content, giving the impression that using the product is slow and restricted. As a result, churn is high and adoption is falling rapidly.

Using the Product VCP, we can begin to outline some initial information:

- **Business objective:** Increase ARR

This is the overall objective for the business - to grow and increase our ARR. As far as business objectives go, this one is probably fairly familiar!

- **Change in behaviour:** Increase the processing of multiple streams of data, taken from the Product VCP.

From here, we now define that one of the behaviours we want to change that in turn help our users find value is to process high volumes of data.

- **Problem statement:** Users don't know that they can process high volumes of data with our system because they're not getting as far as discovering the value of the feature.

With this, we look at the problem and break it down further using a product problem outline, where we start by asking the question, "what problem are we trying to solve?" In this case, we know that users aren't even discovering the feature in question, let alone using it to its full extent.

To use the product problem outline to its full extent, you may look at answering some of the following questions:

- What problem are we trying to solve?
- What's our hypothesis?
- What is the value for the customer?
- What is the value for the business?
- Are there any main action points? (Use this to coordinate stakeholders)
- Do we have any linked documentation or evidence?
- How do we measure success?

With all this information at hand, we can infer that our product objective, in this case, is to improve awareness of the feature. By doing so, we then have the potential to affect an increase in ARR, as per our business objective. This would also give the product team the opportunity to gather feedback about how to possibly improve the solution in the future, given that more customers are now aware of it. By choosing to create awareness first, you're positioning your team to create feedback loops and empower them to learn if the feature has the potential to create more ARR in the future, before spending potential time, money, and resources on a feature that may not have had the behavioural or business impact you were expecting in the first place.

Objective vs. Outcome

While our objective is to improve awareness of the feature, the outcome is not the same. Remember, outcomes must be tied to customer value! In this case, the outcome in mind is to increase the volume of data processing, as that is what will ultimately provide value for your customer base.

The act of adopting is part of the journey to process more data — but the real value lies with the action itself. In order to get users to do the outcome, we must bring awareness to it.

Result: The product objective is to increase awareness of the feature in order to allow users to process more data.

As a second step to this, we might find that users can't process as much data as they wanted to with the existing capability as it currently exists, in which case, this becomes a separate value point. The VCP can enable us to go through this process again and understand the behaviours that we can potentially modify to bring customers value within this particular problem.

Business objective	Value assumption	User behaviour
Increase ARR	Increase processing of	Increase awareness

	multiple streams of data	of features allowing users to process more data
		Reduce user friction when handling multiple data streams
		Increase number of data streams ingested by each user

When we convert this into OKRs, it might look something like this:

Objective (Quantified user behaviour)	Key result (How we measure success)
Increase awareness of features allowing users to process more data resulting in 20% increase of multiple data stream processing (VCP Value Indicator) by the end of Q4	Ensure 100% of new users are educated about data processing capabilities in onboarding
	Proactively suggest to 100% of users who have multiple streams to add other streams
	Achieve 80% user comprehension of how to

	find multiple stream processing features

So if we found that the data capability was underperforming, that becomes a separate objective for the team to tackle.

3: EXPERIMENTING WITH VALUE ASSUMPTIONS

The concept of outcome-driven thinking in B2B SaaS companies coupled with rapid experimentation still feels like a scary and foreign concept for many. With the rapid expansion of the product management field in recent years, change is inevitable — and change can be daunting.

A common concern among founders is the perceived lack of time for experimentation. The pressure to maintain momentum, deliver continuously, and show constant growth and value is significant. But it's important to recognize that growth and value don't just come from releasing things. Constantly shipping features will not avoid the Product Momentum Gap. It is vital to understand why and how something might provide value.

And that's where experimentation comes in. The most frequent objection against running experiments is this: it takes too long. While it might seem that way, experimentation actually provides valuable insights into what to build, and most importantly, what not to build. Rushing to release something without testing viable solutions can lead to building a product nobody wants. This results in wasted time, resources, and finances and incurs tech debt.

Worse, if you've spent money building the wrong thing, you might get trapped trying to make it work rather than discarding it, falling into the sunk cost fallacy where we cling to things simply because we've invested a lot of time in them.

Think of testing product ideas as a way to gauge how your audience might respond to something. If your test proves that your original hypothesis was wrong, you've gained:

1. You've prevented building the wrong thing, thus avoiding various forms of debt.

2. You've learned if solving the problem is feasible.

3. You've gained knowledge about what might work better by finding a better solution or capturing evidence to inform a better solution.

One way to speed up the experimentation process is to see it as a low-code or no-code practice. The primary goal of an experiment is to learn what you might build, not to construct something overly complex, which would defeat the purpose of the process.

This perspective also enables a dual-track agile approach to product development. While your engineering team executes, your product team can focus on quick, low-code experiments, allowing parallel work rather than a single, linear development approach with no room for experimentation.

The continuous cycle of dual-track allows faster movement and the delivery of features and products that address real problems.

Market-leading companies prioritise innovation by putting learning at the forefront of everything they do. These companies celebrate mistakes, adopt new understandings, and have a supporting culture that provides psychological safety for the entire team. This means that asking questions, challenging the status quo, and focusing on what they don't know rather than what they do know is constantly encouraged.

One example is the SaaS company Intercom, which has a hyper-focus on customer success and prioritises moving quickly. In a blog post, an Intercom product manager shares, *"Speeding up customer feedback loops allows you to learn and iterate fast enough to stay ahead of the market while making your customers feel included in the process"*.

A good starting point for this is to allow everyone to discuss the what and why behind new ideas. This cultivates product thinking among all involved and helps the entire organisation understand what it takes to move an idea forward. Encouraging the team to test new ideas rather than merely validating what they think they know eliminates confirmation bias and can reveal better solutions and unforeseen problems. Using the Customer Value Explorer enables your team to step back and ask, *"Do we genuinely understand what value means to our customers?"*

To really promote a culture of experimentation, you have to invest time in discovery. While it might be scary to deviate from the belief that delivering new features equates to delivering value, relentlessly delivering new features doesn't guarantee you're building things people want. A useful product doesn't have to be packed with features.

Often, less is more. It's ok to take a step back and ask the right questions before building something. Output matters, of course it does! — but on the product side of things, we need to take the time to understand user behaviours before we prescribe solutions.

4: TAKING ACCOUNTABILITY

When building products, creating valuable and positive customer experiences should be the company's number one priority. Remember, we're building things for others, not for ourselves. While the idea seems pretty straightforward, there is a difference between "building what people ask for" and "building what people need" — and within that fine line is where the product's purpose exists. If we only build what people ask for, we run a high risk of coming into conflict with the Product Momentum Gap.

The act of creating value from the product team's perspective is formed by three main ingredients:

- Having clarity on company goals

- Having alignment around who your customer & user is

- Solving [the right] customer problems

Have clarity on company goals

At the risk of sounding like a broken record, it all really does boil down to clarity of goals. A clear, solid company vision paves the way for a universally accepted product vision. This, in turn, enables you to devise your overarching strategy, including company goals that everyone can strive towards collectively, thereby eliminating conflicting priorities.

Clear company goals also facilitate measurable product goals and allow for the tracking of impact and progress.

If your work isn't making an impact, it's a strong indication that your solutions might not be creating sufficient value.

Align on who your customer is

More often than not, companies try to please everyone by building features that will, in theory, attract as many customers as possible. But in trying to please everyone, they lose sight of what the product is meant to do and even worse, who it's meant to do it for.

If we refer back to the Product Momentum Gap — we know that trying to rush to create features for everyone is usually what creates the problem in the first place. Instead of attempting to cater to everyone, first establish your product in a specific target market. Once you've made your mark there, you can then extend to adjacent segments.

Solve [the right] problems

Once you have a clear company and product vision and have identified your target audience, you can concentrate on problem-solving. Ask yourself:

- Which initiatives support your company goals?

- Which of those initiatives help reach a customer outcome?

Next, analyse and validate. Where can you experiment further, and what can you learn in order to move forward?

Create and agree on a Product VCP that will allow you to highlight where and how initiatives will have an impact towards your company goals. This will create clarity across the organisation and allow you to remain aligned as you seek to understand which projects with the most impact you can move forward.

Remember, being in product means you're starting off with as many questions as possible. As you start finding answers, there will be less ambiguity as to why and how decisions are made, and allow your entire team to create solutions that deliver value.

5: HOW TO MAKE THIS HAPPEN

Allow us to be blunt: It's time to stop squandering resources by using a roadmap as the primary means of executing your product strategy. It doesn't work.

Product development teams need a strategy that guides them on which problems to solve without prescribing specific features. If we aim to maximise our investment in engineers, designers, and product managers, they must be empowered to understand the root causes of problems and devise the most effective and valuable solutions.

If we simply view them as feature builders, we overlook the real value they bring to the business. This concept is commonly referred to in the product community as "empowered product teams" (see chapter on Organisational Alignment). Empowering your team to take charge is one of the best moves you can make.

The best thing you can do for your product development teams is to empower them to take the reins.

One frequent mistake is to conflate a product strategy with a business strategy, which often fails to align the organisation with what the customer finds valuable. This leaves product managers, engineers, and designers without a clear impact area. The product strategy is often only partially formulated, outlining initiatives or projects tied to business goals but barely hinting at customer value.

Here is a bad example, showing a high-level product strategy focused on business goals:

Business goal	Strategic initiative
Reduce churn	Improve onboarding
	Build integrations
Increase acquisition of enterprise customers	Support SSO

In this example, the business goals take precedence, with strategic initiatives following suit. However, this approach lacks details to help the product team or stakeholders understand what needs improvement. The customer's desired outcome is not conveyed, and the assumptions about how the product might deliver this outcome remain unsaid. What we often see is a list of seemingly valuable features for teams to deliver, a.k.a. a roadmap.

Leadership's aim is to enable teams to execute smoothly and effectively, so providing more clarity is essential.

A roadmap based on the above examples might offer more detailed guidance than the broad strategic initiative of improving onboarding. It might include specific requested features like bulk user creation, a getting started guide, or an interactive guide for each main dashboard. But without evidence or user outcomes clearly outlined, it leads to wasted effort and subpar results. We need to avoid this.

PART FIVE

SELLING VALUE

1: COMMUNICATING VALUE BEYOND THE PRODUCT TEAM

By now you've got your product vision, and you understand how and who you are providing value for with the customer value explorer— excellent! Now, remember to remain transparent and communicate this to your entire organisation. It is impossible to avoid the Product Momentum Gap if only the leadership team understands the value being created.

Many teams struggle with internal communication, especially as companies grow rapidly. It's easy to assume what others know or don't know, and often, the knowledge from the product team isn't shared with the business-facing teams. This can lead to typical organisational communication issues such as:

- Marketing talking about a product that doesn't exist.

- Sales incorrectly selling features that don't match the capabilities of the product.

- Customer Success struggling to maintain strong relationships with customers.

All of these problems can absolutely be avoided, and all it takes is to switch the team mindset from talking at each other to talking with each other.

This means changing the context from:

We've built feature x, it does these things and will go live next week.

To:

We have built feature x, which helps customers reach **[a specific outcome.]**

This serves **[customer segment]** in our product vision,

provides **[this particular experience]**, influences these **[behaviours]**

And aligns **[with company goal x]** and impacts this **[key result.]**

Due to the pressure to release quickly, communication often resembles the first scenario, which doesn't help anyone understand why and how it benefits customers. It is less effort to talk about what you have done rather than why you did it.

Taking an extra few moments to add more context around what, why, for whom, and how it's related to the overall strategy is an absolute game changer and will provide support for your external facing teams to have better conversations.

Your roadmap, strategy, and product vision should also be communicated as part of your decision-making presentation. There is often fear around information being "leaked" or team members misinterpreting the roadmap. The real concern should be the lack of communication. With transparency leading the way, you're reducing unwanted situations that crop up: sales incorrectly selling features, marketing mis-selling the value prop, and angry customers on both sides of the aisle. The clearer you are about your direction and intention for the product, the more you will be able to influence those around you.

Another way to communicate value outwards is by building a Product Value Pyramid that outlines the outcomes of the Product VCP so that the results are easy to visualise.

The Pyramid would comprise of the following:

- **Whose life are we improving?** This is your intended audience. Outline use cases, sectors, roles, and industries impacted.

- **What is the problem that we solve?** Highlight the main problems you are aiming to solve, including the main challenges and potential opportunities you have.

- **Why is this important?** These are your value indicators. Why are these things important to your users?

- **What is the experience we want to provide?** What do you want your customers to take away after using your product? How are you positioned to provide those experiences?

- **What behaviours do we want to influence?** These are the identified behaviours from the Product VCP that will influence better habits.

The Product Value Pyramid is illustrated below.

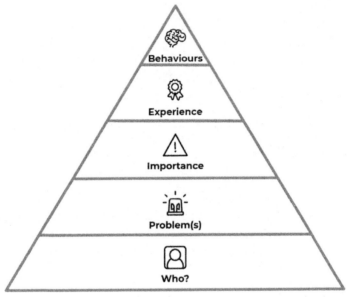

Figure 7 Product Value Pyramid

2: ACHIEVING AND MAINTAINING CUSTOMER TRACTION

Determining whether your product meets market demand is just the first step toward success. But what happens after? What do you do when you start gaining traction? Most importantly: When do you revise your viability and positioning within the market and open yourself to continue growing, learning, or even pivoting?

The short answer: always.

Product-market fit is not binary, nor is it static. It's a dynamic journey of growth and learning, where understanding the evolving market landscape helps you adapt to your customers' changing needs.

Outpacing the competition isn't about being first to market. Numerous companies have launched innovative products only to be surpassed by competitors who delivered later but better. The Apple iPhone has consistently delivered features after Android phones have, yet their marketing communicates a specific set of values that connect with their user base, making them extremely loyal to the brand.

Getting ahead means being able to identify gaps in the market and addressing those in a manner that is unique to the problem you are solving. Teams often get distracted by shiny object syndrome, thinking that they must offer that exact same feature their competitor just released. That never works. "Feature parity" is in no way a strategy.

While there may or may not be some truth to their

particular new feature being a need for customers, the only product way you will get ahead is by identifying what the problem is in the market and finding a better customer experience to solve it. Trying to reach feature parity with another company is not always the best strategy — you do not know the internal justification they had for building that particular thing. Do not be fooled into believing larger companies have already collected [the right] evidence to proceed with something. Often, larger companies have more money to waste, and they can afford to have failed products. While it may be a good idea on the surface, the way to get ahead is to recognize that 1, there is a problem and 2, you have a better way of solving it.

And this brings us to our next point. How do you know how to solve a problem better than someone else?

A better understanding of customer problems will give you the advantage to solve problems better. By creating feedback loops, having higher learning velocity, and using that to iterate. Continuous growth and learning come from listening to your market. Most importantly, it comes from the understanding that you do not know it all.

As we've said before: it's ok to be wrong; that is how we learn! Constantly challenging your assumptions, testing, iterating, and listening is what will give you the edge you are looking for. Of course, the flip side to that is knowing that it is also ok to say no to some things, and that will come from understanding your product, market, and vision well. Products fail when they don't solve the right problem or when they're trying to solve *too many* problems at the same time. This can be challenging for founders who have a vision with billions of dollars of potential and desire to act on all aspects immediately. The product strategy executed with the Product VCP is crucial to support the founder, so the value is realised for the customer and the company on the journey towards the big picture.

It's important to have a solid grasp on market needs, just as much as it is important to have a solid grasp on who your target audience actually is. And with that, we come to another important point: scaling. In order to scale successfully, you have to be clear about who your ideal customer is and how best positioned you might be to provide them with a specific set of values.

Many companies start building software for small companies, and as they shift towards growth, they will start moving up to cater to enterprises. Here's the thing: startups and enterprises do not have the same needs or problems, so you're going to have to make a choice. Otherwise, you'll end up with everyone's least favourite problem: feature bloat.

We can, of course, combat some of this with Product-Led Growth. PLG allows us to carve out a path for our customers as their own companies grow and mature. As their needs change, the possibilities and values your product offers then expand to meet those needs. Yet, at some point, you will find yourself having to decide where your team's focus on delivering value will be.

The most successful products are those that do one thing and do it right. Be fierce about your vision, your customers, your goals, and your market — and don't let anyone come in between that. When you try to do it all, you fail at most things. Add focus in order to grow steadily, and don't get distracted by things that, on the outside, only appear to be working for others.

Paul Graham once said, *"Most startups fail because they're solving problems that nobody has."*

Fact is, he's right.

Companies often fail because they didn't take the time to understand if the product they are building is solving real-world problems. Does anyone remember Juicero? The Guardian wrote: *"the absurd Silicon Valley startup industry that raises huge sums of money for solutions to non-problems".* (1)

With that in mind, the term "validation" is a bit of a two-edged sword. While the idea behind it is to understand if the product you're building will solve customer needs, a lot of people take the word "validation" as the process of proving themselves right. Validation is about testing and understanding where your product solves a problem, where it does not, and what gaps you can potentially fill to truly find a competitive edge. It does not mean going out and proving that you're right — because the reality is, most of the time, you might not be. If your experiments are always proving you right, you should take the time to question that.

Not being right is the best thing that can happen to any product leader or founder. It means you have the opportunity to learn things you weren't previously aware of and even find ways to solve problems that you hadn't thought of before.

As you're getting ready to validate your vision, strategy, and even your fit in the market, remember you're not there to prove yourself right. Instead, open up to the possibility that there are a lot of things you might not know — and understanding those will help you build a better product.

A good way to focus on solving the right problems is by asking two really simple questions: What problem are we solving, and why might this be important to the customer? (Refer to the product problem outline.) Supplement this with research and feedback, and determine the best solution for your wider audience.

In other words, don't build features for a single customer, but solve problems for your intended market. By using the product VCP, you can make decisions based on the market instead of a single individual. This is what leads to hyper-growth instead of stagnation.

How it all fits together

Let's use a couple of example scenarios to illustrate what we've learned so far.

Scenario 1:

Suppose we're developing an app aimed at streamlining workforce planning, specifically targeting users who schedule warehouse staff. Our goal is to enable faster and fairer scheduling.

- **Intended audience:** Warehouse workforce schedulers.

- **User behaviour:** Weekly schedule creation. Our goal is to modify this behaviour to increase speed and reduce accidental bias, thereby improving fairness.

- **Customer value:** For schedulers and warehouse staff alike, enhanced job retention could be a valuable outcome.

Scenario 2:

For this example, let's imagine we're a company offering e-marketing software for e-commerce marketers.

- **Intended audience:** E-commerce marketers

- **User behaviour:** Execution of targeted email campaigns. We want to modify this behaviour to extend the campaigns' reach without diminishing their relevancy.

- **Customer value:** Improved campaign effectiveness, possibly reflected in higher click-through rates, could lead to increased revenue, a significant benefit for customers.

Having identified the behaviour we aim to influence and hypothesised the potential value for the customer, the next step involves research. We need to explore our assumptions, the projected value, and potential solutions to the problem at hand.

A product strategy can highlight opportunities and potential problems to be solved. However, without considering the factors that influence behaviour, user experience, and customer value, we risk missing the mark in our strategic execution. Our ultimate goal is to leverage these insights to create truly remarkable products.

Source:
(1)https://web.archive.org/web/20210426070347/https://www.theguardian.com/technology/2017/sep/01/jui

cero-silicon-valley-shutting-down

3: MASTERING PRODUCT POSITIONING

Finding the right product positioning can be challenging. You need to provide value for your customers, but also make sure you're differentiating yourself enough with a unique value proposition against your competitors. Founders might be concerned the positioning will reduce their market size and impact investor appetite.

When companies with a good product are struggling to grow it can often be they are positioned towards the wrong market. This can give the perception that you don't have the right product when in reality you might have a great product — you're just selling to the wrong market.

The Product Momentum Gap happens when you expand the market too fast before you've had the chance to establish yourself within an existing market. While your product might solve a problem in Market A and Market B, remember: capabilities remain constant; positioning pivots. As we've established, product-market fit is a journey, a principle that applies to both your current and future markets.

As we've discussed before, the idea of customer traction and "fit" is a continuous journey, and this applies to both your existing market but also potential ones you might have in the future. Your product should focus on solving problems and addressing use cases, not necessarily just for a set of personas.

Personas are useful, but the discussion of their significance merits a separate conversation. They help us understand how to speak to different audiences about the use cases that solve a variety of problems for them.

Make sure that you have an understanding of the problem you solve, that is, the what and why, who you solve it for, outlined with your personas, and where your unique value proposition is using the Product VCP. This will help you break into new markets and continue to solidify your market share.

Revisiting the Product Value Pyramid, we see how it aids in our positioning. It encapsulates our intended audience, relevant sectors, use cases, problems we solve, customer perceptions, desired experience, and behaviours we aim to influence.

In it, we have:

- Our intended audience

    o The relevant sectors/industries

- Use cases

- What problems we solve for them

- Their perception of why this is important

- Experience we want to provide

- Behaviours we want to change

With this, the Product VCP helps us with our positioning and messaging, without having to create entirely new capabilities for a new market that will inevitably result in feature bloat.

If you're wondering at this point: why does this matter? Is this not product marketing's problem? Can I not hand this off to my marketing team?

Product marketing is product. Your product marketing team is there to be your strategic partner and the communication side of everything you do. Lean on them to help define your Product VCP and socialise it across the organisation. Product is also the best-positioned function to recognize the problem in different markets.

Whereas your marketing team will look at how to message and communicate with different verticals and find common language in different industries — it is up to the product to recognize where the problem exists. Once the problem is recognised, the next step is to understand the context in which your product might be helpful to a specific audience, understand the values customers are looking for, and research the types of behaviours your product might be able to improve.

As a product leader, you'll be a lot more equipped to lead your team into new territory. However, instead of approaching it blindly, you'll be armed with all the information you need to expand into new markets and close that Product Momentum Gap that much faster.

Let's take a closer look at how you can work with your marketing team on product positioning.

Your product should have anywhere between 1-5 use cases, at least to start with, for your intended audience. Use cases are the problems that you solve at a really high level.

Let's pretend that we're positioning an email marketing platform, with our intended audience being email marketers.

Our top three use cases given this scenario might be:

- To send newsletters

- To send email campaigns

- To send targeted emails to a segment of a mailing list

This is just our starting point. Now the product team can outline some key tasks for the marketing team.

As an email marketer, given that....I want to send newsletters, in order to.....

Repeat the same exercise a few times and outline the outcome for your email marketing persona for each problem you're solving. Tap into those behaviours to assist your marketing team in additional messages that will tackle those behaviour changes from the beginning of their experience with your brand, not just within your product. This will provide a platform for positioning, messaging, and marketing material for your entire team.

As you can see, this is not an exercise you do in a silo - it is an exercise that should be done with your marketing team. Product leaders in a B2B space must have a commercial focus at all times, and it is your job to promote that cross-team collaboration with your marketing, sales, and customer success teams. A big part of product management is being able to sell value. Instead of complaining that "they don't get what we're doing," we can make an effort to communicate and work with them on what they need to be successful.

Of course, communication goes beyond this single exercise. Remember to also work with your commercial teams on the product VCP, when sharing decisions about what and why, and of course, your roadmap. As part of your leadership role, you also need to lead commercial teams and support them in their success.

4: REDEFINING POSITIONING WITH THE VCP

To bring this all together, let's consider a real example of a product leader embracing the Product VCP to support market positioning.

Johanna joined a B2B startup post series-A at a time when they were trying to reposition their offering in the market. Her main job was to ensure the repositioning made the company stand out in a saturated market and establish itself as a serious competitor. Above all, the main issue the company had was that customers didn't understand what they were offering, and how the product was different from its competitors.

Before Johanna's start, the marketing team had identified half a dozen personas across multiple markets, for which they wanted to create specific landing pages and user journeys for. That's quite a lot of work!

Johanna quickly noticed the team was misaligned around who the intended audience was, including marketing, sales, success, and product. To fix the alignment issue, she chose to use the Product Value Pyramid.

Before getting to the pyramid though, there was an inherent issue with the product strategy: there wasn't one!

After a few workshops and meetings with the leadership team, they were able to come to a consensus about the strategy and value proposition. This allowed the team to focus on who their market was, removing the notion of specific personas. With this now set, they were able to reduce down to a handful of customer segments.

Once the behaviours and experiences had been agreed upon in a separate workshop with the product team, Johanna put together all of the information for the organisation and made it visible to everyone. This ensured transparency and opened up communication beyond just the product team. Most importantly, this exercise highlighted to leadership that there were still too many customer segments to approach, so they decided to keep just one and really solidify their state in the market. With one very clear market segment, they could start focusing on building and communicating value accordingly.

Instead of building specific user journeys for personas within the agreed upon market segment, the team decided to take this opportunity to learn from their value assumptions.

Step 1: Communicate value through use cases.

Instead of creating landing pages for personas (for example for marketing teams,) they decided to build landing pages built on pain points, like "Expedite content creation". This would give the team the opportunity to communicate value and benefits based on a particular problem, rather than risk alienating other "personas" within the market that may be interested in the value they provide.

A great example of another well-known company that does this is Figma. Their use cases include prototyping, wireframing, designing, and brainstorming - to name a few - but they don't specifically call out that their solutions are for designers only. Their positioning is that their product is for teams to get involved in the design process, and they can co-create (with designers) in one space.

Step 2: Validating decisions

The second clear step here was to validate that the use cases were the correct ones after all. Remember, at the end of the day these are value assumptions, and they need to be tested to see if they align with the strategy and are providing the expected outcome.

To understand if they were moving in the right direction, the team implemented a quick survey at the beginning of the user journey asking a few quick questions about the organisation, including industry, company size, and what their expected outcome was from using the product.

Because they had the Product Value Pyramid at hand, the marketing team was able to position the use cases on the website to highlight the value and set the change in behaviour and experience before the user started their trial. Once their trial kicked off, the product team was able to tie in that experience into the product and set up onboarding journeys that supported the continuation of that change/adaptation of behaviour — while still proceeding to learn from their market.

The result? An increase of over 60% in site visitors on a rolling monthly basis. Meanwhile, their conversion rate from site visitor to trialist doubled. Focusing on problems rather than personas shifted the perception of the audience, resulting in a bigger impact.

And that wasn't the only side effect of making the Product Value Pyramid available to everyone. The team was also able to create valuable assets for sales and customer success that focused on communicating those value points and created that change in behaviour. Now product, sales, marketing, and customer success were all communicating the same message to their customers as a unified chorus.

5: HOW TO MAKE THIS HAPPEN

The leadership team needs to ensure that the value assumptions defined remain consistent and true throughout the organisation. Use them to align not just positioning, but the marketing and sales teams with the product. Allow marketing and sales to position the messaging as needed, but ensure that these are mapped back to the original set of value assumptions. This is where your product marketing team will be essential!

As product leaders, we know the behaviours we are trying to create that will generate value for the customer. The positioning of the product needs to have those value assumptions at the heart of it.

We can frame those value assumptions in different ways for different customers, but they must remain the same. If the value assumption changes, are we still communicating the value of our product in a way that remains true?

The key here is alignment. To quote April Dunford on a recent appearance on Lenny's Podcast: "Weak positioning comes from lack of alignment across various departments." Alignment above all must be the driver here - but be willing to take learnings and challenges from everyone. Leading value indicators are there to be reviewed periodically. If these go up, it means we are positively creating those behaviours in our users. If we are not, be open to talk with your team about where you might be able to make changes. Remember, it's always better to have strong beliefs loosely held.

PART SIX

PRODUCT VCP TOOLKIT

Customer Value Mapper™

Business objective:

Business objective:

Business objective:

Customer value:

Customer value:

Customer value:

Customer value:

Why?:

Why?:

Why?:

Why?:

Customer Value Explorer™

Customer value:

How would the customer recognise this?:

What customer KPI changes?:

What customer actions or behaviours impact the value?:

How could Product improve this?:

Are we best positioned to create this value?:

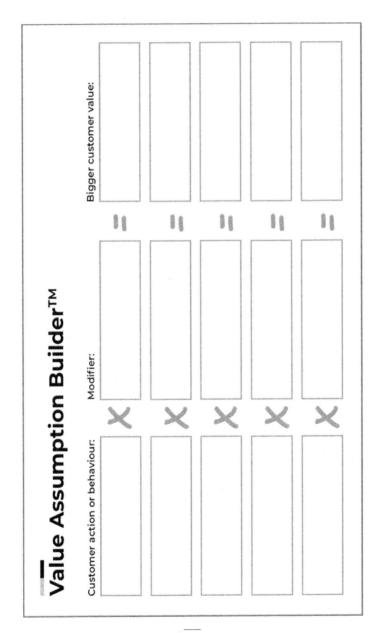

Value Assumption Builder™

Customer action or behaviour: Modifier: Bigger customer value:

Value Indicator Chooser™

Customer action or behaviour:	What is the measurable value outcome?:	Is this a lead or lag metric?:

Leading indicators:	Can our product impact this?:	Can we measure this?:

Chosen value indicator:

Product Value Creation Tracker™

Date upadted:

Value indicator:	Current performance:	Target:	Last 4 week delta:	Trend:

Strategic Value Matrix™

Value indicators:

								Total

Strategic bets:

Audeince Explorer™

Who?:

Sector:

Sector:

Sector:

Sector:

Job titles:

Jobs to be done:

Audeince Perception Explorer™

For:

Customer value:

HINT refer to The Customer Value Explorer.

Their problem:

Their importance:

Desired experience:

Desired behaviour:

ACKNOWLEDGEMENTS

We were lucky enough to have enjoyed support and advice with the process of writing this book. We already mentioned of John Cutler, C. Todd Lombardo, Kate Leto who provided enormous support with the manuscript. We must thank Hayley Martin for all the support and the design of the book and cover.

We also want to thank those that help with editing, publishing advice and morale support! This includes Thom Oliver, Michaela Heigl, Phil Hornby, Randy Silver, April Dunford, Petra Wille, David Peto, Nacho Bassino, and Tara Halliday.

ACKNOWLEDGEMENTS

We were lucky enough to have enjoyed support and advice with the process of writing this book. We already mentioned of John Cutler, C. Todd Lombardo, Kate Leto who provided enormous support with the manuscript. We must thank Hayley Martin for all the support and the design of the book and cover.

We also want to thank those that help with editing, publishing advice and morale support! This includes Thom Oliver, Michaela Heigl, Phil Hornby, Randy Silver, April Dunford, Petra Wille, David Peto, Nacho Bassino, and Tara Halliday.